ROBERT DEGROOT

Value Selling Strategies

P.R.O.S.P.E.C.T. Model

First published by Robert DeGroot 1995

Author's note: Scripts and stories in this book are based on actual events but are modified for clarity, continuity, and privacy.

61124(2)

For rights and permissions, please contact:

ROBERT DEGROOT

Bob@SalesHelp.com

https://SalesHelp.com

Fifth edition

ISBN: 9780986405891

This book was professionally typeset on Reedsy.
Find out more at reedsy.com

Contents

1

Introduction to Value Selling Strategies

In the Value Selling Strategies (VSS) process, the actual selling is done during a strategically designed interview structured around major closing strategies. It is designed to PREVENT most common sales-stopping objectives. It does this by establishing each of the critical Buyer Beliefs that, when missing or weak, cause objections.

Selling VALUE gets easier with the right tools and an incredibly flexible structure to guide the process. The Value Selling Strategies P.R.O.S.P.E.C.T. Model™ (VSS) provides the latest knowledge, skills, and strategies to accomplish this goal.

- Use a sales interaction model guided by the psychological buying process.
- Qualify and disqualify prospects based on the profile of your most profitable customers.
- Identify the fundamental buying influences and decision-makers.
- Guide the prospect to discover the value of your products and services.
- Avoid common pitfalls of presenting solutions after discovering needs.
- Move the pressure of time and priority from you to the prospect.
- Prevent most common objections, especially price.
- Help the prospect set the product/service selection criteria (specifications).
- Identify your unique selling points in each sales situation.

- Work with a list of 80 areas where commodity sellers differentiate themselves.
- Be forewarned about which objections you must neutralize.
- Include your unique selling points in the selection buying criteria.
- Help the prospect rule out and lock out the competition for you.
- Discover priority buying motives.
- Let the prospect make the "claims" for the benefits rather than you.
- Rehearse the prospect to sell internally for you when you're not around.
- Create change-resistant attitudes favorable to your unique selling points.
- Structure your sales interaction around major closing strategies.
- Block the competition between calls with three techniques.
- Use the Customer Value Proposition (CVP) to establish trust and rapport with those you didn't meet during the sales interviewing process.
- Present your product/service to the prospect's selected criteria.
- Structure your presentation around major closing strategies.

Rationale: An Intensely Competitive Marketplace

This value selling model is specifically designed for those who sell higher-priced solutions to their customers' problems and do so in an intensely competitive market.

For most sellers, "Consultative Value Selling" models provide the core selling skills needed to thrive in this environment. The more intense the competition, the more sellers lean toward models, enabling them to understand their competitors differently and use that knowledge to win sales where preventable objections stop others.

The Value Selling Strategies P.R.O.S.P.E.C.T. Model (VSS) is structured to establish each of the critical 10 Buyer Beliefs that, when missing or weak, cause your objections. Every day, sales professionals use this model to prevent objections from stopping or stalling their sales.

Missing or weak Buyer Beliefs Cause Objections

What causes the objections you get? Simply, the prospect doesn't have one or more key beliefs they must have before they buy.

Research with thousands of salespeople across industries demonstrates the following:

- Objections that stop almost all sales are common and repetitive.
- Specific Buyer Beliefs, when missing or weak, cause these objections.
- There are many ways to establish these beliefs to prevent the objection from entering the prospect's mind.

Test this:

- Before you buy something, this book, for example, ask, "What's one thing must you believe about it?"
- If you don't believe that, what objection comes to mind?
- But, if you did believe that, what happens to the objection?
- You just demonstrated that a missing Buyer Belief caused the objection and that when the belief is in place, the objection goes away.

Analysis reveals:

- There are ten critical Buyer Beliefs in which all sales objections can be categorized.
- Salespeople get most of their objections in three to five categories of missing Buyer Beliefs.
- Learning how to prevent, preempt, and respond to a few objections in each category will handle all objections in that category.
- It doesn't matter which sales model salespeople use if sales-stopping objections are getting through.
- The strategies and formulas provided work with all sales models.

To be motivated to carry out any activity, whether going to a movie or buying something you want or need, the decision to take action is based on your beliefs. Those beliefs trigger emotions, and emotions provide the energy to move forward.

When an objection comes up, it tells us that at least one of the buyer's beliefs is not entirely in place. The objection itself tells us which of the buyer's beliefs is missing. The information below lists and briefly describes each of the ten buyer beliefs, and across from each belief are examples of objections associated with them.

Buyer Beliefs

Buyer Belief 1: Need Exists

A need is a gap between the current situation (problem) and a more desirable condition (solution). Related objections when the belief that a "need exists" is missing:

- *Not interested.*
- *Already have someone.*
- *Don't need it.*

Buyer Belief 2: Responsibility

The person has or shares the responsibility to fill the need. Related objections when the belief "responsibility" is missing:

- *I'm only getting the information for my boss.*
- *My job is to qualify suppliers.*

Buyer Belief 3: Authority

The person has or shares the authority to fill the need. Related objections when the belief "authority" is missing:

- *I need to talk with my ______ before I can make that decision.*

- *My boss won't authorize* anything.

The Buyer Beliefs "Responsibility" and "Authority" are combined going forward in this book because the preventing, preempting, and responding strategies are essentially the same. They will be addressed separately when the strategies are not the same.

Buyer Belief 4: Discomfort Felt

The prospect's needs are strong enough to cause discomfort. The gain (benefit) is strong enough to motivate moving forward. Related objections when the belief "discomfort felt" is missing:

- *Just send me your literature.*
- *Don't have time to discuss it now.*
- *We'll get by with what we have now.*

Buyer Belief 5: Need has Priority

The discomfort felt is painful enough, or the gain is sufficient to prioritize this need over other needs. Related objections when the belief "need has priority" is missing:

- *No money in the budget; call me next year.*
- *We have too many other things in front of this.*
- *We need to think this over.*

Buyer Belief 6: Type of Solution

The prospect believes your type of solution will successfully satisfy their needs. Related objections when the belief "type of solution" is missing:

- *We've never had good results with _____.*
- *You don't have what we need.*
- *I need a quality that is better than what you offer.*

Buyer Belief 7: Capability and Credibility

You, your product, service, and company have the capability and credibility to satisfy the need. You have the necessary levels of trust and rapport. Related objections when the belief "capability and credibility" is missing:

- *We want someone in our industry.*
- *How do you know it will do that?*
- *I've never heard of your company.*

Buyer Belief 8: Best Solution

Your solution, to the exclusion of competing solutions, will best satisfy the need. Related objections when the belief "best solution" is missing:

- *Don't see any reason to change.*
- *Why should I buy from you?*
- *I am happy with what I am buying now.*

Buyer Belief 9: Return on Investment

The price of the solution is less than the cost of the problem. Costs can be financial, subjective (hassle), or emotional (frustration). Related objections when the belief about "ROI" is missing:

- *Your price is too high.*
- *I don't have the time (subjective value).*
- *Not in the budget.*

Buyer Belief 10: Plan Will Succeed

Your plan to meet the need will succeed. Related objections when the belief "plan will succeed" is missing:

- *They will never buy into it.*
- *It's too much trouble to change.*
- *This is a lot to think about.*

Think about the last sale you lost. Can you identify which Buyer Belief(s) were weak or missing?

Now, think about a sale you won. Can you identify any Buyer Beliefs that were weak or missing, regardless of whether you put them in place or not? In a business setting, what is the probability the decision-makers (team) would have bought without having all ten beliefs?

Selling is about putting each Buyer's Belief in place with your prospects. When you establish each belief, the corresponding objections are less likely to occur. The question-based VSS P.R.O.S.P.E.C.T. Model is designed to put these beliefs in place.

P.R.O.S.P.E.C.T. Model Establishes Buyer Beliefs to Prevent Objections

P - Profile: Profile Questions qualify the prospect and identify the buying influences. This component addresses Buyer Beliefs of Responsibility and Authority.

R - Research: Research Questions gain vital customer and competitor information to develop a win/win sales strategy. This category of questions provides strategies for identifying areas where you're strong and the competitor is weak. These are your Unique Selling Points (USPs) that meet needs only you can fill. This category also guides you in confirming that your customer has these needs.

O - Orientation: Orientation Questions activate your sales strategy by focusing the conversation on areas where you are strong, your competitor is weak, and the prospect has needs. Calls attention to one side of the gap (need).

S - Symptom: The Symptom Question intends to identify the obvious and the hidden needs not currently met by the competitor. Substantiates that a gap exists through recognizing the feeling of discomfort and, by inference, the desire for something better (solution). The more areas you can orient the prospect to find symptoms of not having your Unique Selling Points, the greater the pain (or gain) and the higher the priority.

P - Problem: The Problem Question identifies the root causes of the symptoms and confirms the problems' existence. It names the problem side of the gap and points to the solution.

E - Effects/Consequences: The Effects Consequences Question quantifies what it costs the customer not to have the advantages and benefits of your Unique Selling Points. Effects questions look at past and present costs, and the Consequences question looks at future costs. This is how you establish the value of your solution. When using Unique Selling Points to establish value, you are also helping to reduce price pressure by demonstrating a "bottom-line" cost advantage. Determines the size of the gap by quantifying the cost of the problem. Helps to establish the value of the solution. It demonstrates that your Return on Investment (ROI) exceeds the competitor's.

C - Criteria/Benefits: The Criteria/Benefits Questions get agreement on the criteria that must be met to solve the problems and get the prospect to rehearse a defense for the criteria. These questions establish the other side of the gap to establish the need. The more needs you can establish using your Unique Selling Points (USPs), the more the customer rules out the competitor as unable to meet their needs, and the higher your Capability and Credibility will rise. Structuring your criteria in the persuasive language of selling (Features, Advantages, Benefits) demonstrates that your "Type of Solution" is the one that will work to meet their defined needs. Since your solution is the only solution that can fill the needs identified with your Unique Selling Points, your solution is the best solution to satisfy all the needs.

T - Triggering Events: The Triggering Events Questions help you and the prospect develop a win/win plan of action to achieve customer satisfaction. Establishes the "Plan of Action" Buyer Belief.

Buyer Belief Categories to P.R.O.S.P.E.C.T. Question Categories

It is essential to understand the psychology of how buyers buy to appreciate how this model becomes so exceptionally powerful. Let's begin with what a buyer must believe to some extent before making a purchase.

Let's work this process backward because, as you now know, each of these beliefs must be established to some degree of strength, or an objection specific to that belief will occur, spoken or not.

There are many ways to establish each of these Buyer Beliefs. The P.R.O.S.P.E.C.T. Model is one way to assemble action categories that systematically establish all the Buyer Beliefs through questions in an easy-to-remember formula.

Need Exists: The "gap" is established when the **P**roblem is identified and the **C**riteria for the solution is agreed upon. You get to substantiate the problem's existence by first **O**rienting the prospect to one of your Unique Selling Point's Features, then asking about the missing Advantages and Benefits or the **S**ymptoms of not having the Feature.

Responsibility and Authority: The **P**rofile questions help you identify the buying influences.

Discomfort Felt: This is the pain or gain component. What are their greatest concerns about not having the Advantages and Benefits your Unique Selling Points (USPs) Features provide? What could they gain by getting them?

Need has Priority: The more **S**ymptoms you uncover for a single Unique Selling Point's Feature, Advantage, and Benefits, and the more Unique Selling Points you discuss using the P.R.O.S.P.E.C.T. Model, the higher the priority need fulfillment becomes. Additionally, the more money you can quantify being lost due to not having your Unique Selling Points capabilities

(Effects/Consequences), the higher the pressure they feel about moving forward.

Type of Solution: Since these Unique Selling Points (USPs) follow an irrefutable "this, then that" logic with the Features (this), Advantages, and Benefits (then that), your type of solution will obviously work to provide the missing Advantages and Benefits. For example, if the prospect uses containers that rust and the replacement budget is growing, then buying containers made of (F) plastic, (A) that won't rust, (B) will reduce the replacement budget eventually to zero (for rust issues). This is circular logic, and it becomes self-proving.

Capability and Credibility: Driving the sales process with questions shifts the pressure to prove the statements to the person making them. Additionally, if you ask the prospect about the Benefits they think they'll get during the Criteria/Benefit questions, they are making the claims, not you. The person giving the answers and making the claims has the burden of proof. Again, the circular logic used with your Unique Selling Points provides Capability and Credibility.

Best Solution: Once your Unique Selling Points are set as part of the Criteria, specifications, requirements, or objectives (written or not), then you will have the only solution that will fill their needs. Using this process helps the customer rule out your competition.

Return on Investment (ROI): Quantifying the value of your USPs' Advantages and Benefits will show that your ROI is greater than your competitor's. The initial numbers can also be projected into the future for the length of the service agreement or the product's expected life.

Plan of Action: One event triggers the next. The Triggering Events "advance the sale" using closing strategies such as the Agenda Close, the Next Step Close, the Plan of Action Close, the Interim Action Close, and others. Decision-makers who are not familiar with buying what you sell or don't have experience with your organization will have a higher anxiety level. Consequently, the steps in your Plan of Action must be smaller and more detailed than needed with someone who knows and trusts you.

P.R.O.S.P.E.C.T. / F.A.B. Formula

The VSS P.R.O.S.P.E.C.T. Model is fully integrated with your product, service, and company knowledge expressed as Features, Advantages, and Benefits (FAB). What people pay for are the Features that provide the Advantages and Benefits that fill needs.

What we sell determines whom we sell to and helps us establish the **Profile** of our customers.

What we look for in conducting our **Research** is to discover how our Unique Selling Points (USP) can help the prospect one or more of their business needs better than our competitors can.

We **Orient** the prospective customer to areas where we are strong and the competitor is weak (use the Features of your unique selling points).

The **Symptoms** we find are the "missing" Advantages and Benefits of our Unique Selling Point's Feature. It is what you look for when someone does not have the Advantages and Benefits of your USPs.

The **Problem** is defined as the missing Feature because if they had your USP Feature, they would have its Advantages and Benefits, and consequently, there would be no Symptoms in this area. But since they have the Symptoms, they don't have your USP Feature, and that's the problem, right?

The **Effects/Consequences** are the quantification of what it costs (subjective, emotional, and financial) for the customer not to have your Unique Selling Point's Advantages and Benefits now (Effects) or in the future (Consequences).

The **Criteria** you set are your Features. You then explain these Features with their Advantages and Benefits.

The **Triggering Events** are the logistical steps necessary for the prospect to own what we sell.

The connection between your product, service, and company knowledge and the VSS P.R.O.S.P.E.C.T. Model should begin to be clear. We'll discuss this critical linkage in detail in those modules that are directly involved.

P.R.O.S.P.E.C.T. Model in Action

Case Study: The Jill Ryan Scenario

The "Jill Ryan" case study will help illustrate the model. Throughout this book, we'll use the Jill Ryan scenario for consistency and ease of learning.

Consider that what Jill Ryan sells is considered a commodity. That means she must use differentiation based on how her company provides the service and does business. You, too, can do the same thing: focus more on how you and your company do business rather than on the product or service itself.

Jill Ryan sells a repair service for electronic motor control systems that adjust the amount of energy the conveyor belt motor needs to maintain a steady speed under different loads.

In developing a profile of her most desirable customers, she found they had several common characteristics:

- They are in the manufacturing, food processing, and distribution industries.
- They use multiple, individually controlled conveyor systems.
- They run 24-hour operations.
- Their facilities are not climate-controlled or have wet wash downs of the equipment.
- Many of the motor controllers are still under warranty
- The Final Authority is usually the Vice-President of Operations.

Research shows that Jill faces two competitors in her territory that offer the same service for a much lower price. Her company charges $125 per service hour, while her competitors charge $80.00 per hour. According to Jill's "competitor analysis," neither offers 24-hour service with 7-day service availability as her company does. This capability could be important if equipment goes down after regular work hours or on the weekends.

- **Feature:** 24-hour service, 7 days a week
- **Advantage:** Service available after regular work hours
- **Benefit:** Less downtime for after-hour repairs

Pre-call planning: Jill has a referral to Mr. John Simms, VP of Operations. In preparation for her call, she jots down her key information.

Orientation: Repair service hours of operation.

Symptoms: Production downtime after hours and on weekends - waiting for regular business hours so repairs can occur, lost production from waiting, plus actual repair time.

Problem: Not having 24-hour, 7-day service.

Effects / Consequences: Cost of downtime to be budgeted during the next 12 months.

Criteria / Benefits: 24-hour service, seven days a week, to provide service when needed to reduce the cost of excessive (waiting) downtime, per the prospect's personal and inside knowledge of others' needs.

Triggering Events: Meet with the prospect to explore this and other issues that Jill's company can offer other unique selling points.

Jill gets John Simms on the phone. Let's see what happens.

Simms: *"This is John Simms."*

Jill: *"Mr. Simms, I'm Jill Ryan with ECS Repair Service. Good morning."*

Simms: *"Good morning. How can I help you?"*

Jill: *"I'm calling because Bill Smith suggested I talk with you about how we helped his company solve some of the costly and critical issues related to electronic control system repair. He said you were probably facing the same challenges they were. Is now a good time to verify some quick information, or should we set a telephone appointment for later today?"*

Simms: *"Now would be okay. And I like the past tense comment when you said 'they were having.'"*

Jill: **[Profile]** *"Mr. Simms, I understand you are operating seven conveyor* *systems around the clock."*

Simms: *"That's right."*

Jill: **[Research]** *"Who are you currently using for your electronic control system repair?"*

Simms: *"We've been using Hardware Inc. for many years."*

Jill: **[Orientation]** *"I'd like to focus for a moment in the area of repair service hours of operation,* [**Symptom**] *what is your greatest area of concern when your control system goes down after regular business hours or on the weekend?"*

Simms: *"The biggest headache is downtime on the equipment. We can lose a lot of production."*

Jill: **[Symptom]** *"Is that due to the repair time or service availability?"*

Simms: *"The actual repair time is usually only an hour or two, but having to wait for our contract service to get here the next day is where the time really adds up."*

Jill: **[Problem]** *"So that points to a problem with not having repair service availability around the clock and on weekends, doesn't it?"*

Simms: *"Yes, I guess it is."*

Jill: **[Effects]** *"How often are the control systems going down after hours or on the weekend?"*

Simms: *"Two or three times a month, we operate in a pretty hostile environment here."*

Jill: **[Effects]** *"How many hours are you down over the actual repair time?"*

Simms: *"My last set of figures shows we're losing about 9 hours of production per month waiting for the repair service, which seems to be growing over what we experienced last year."*

Jill: **[Effects]** *"What would you estimate the cost of an hour of production?"*

Simms: *"Each hour of production is about $250."*

Jill: **[Effects]** *"9 hours per month at $250 per hour would bring the actual cost to $2,250 per month that would have to be factored into the repair service budget."*

Simms: *"That's just about right."*

Jill: **[Effects]** *"What does that amount do to the per-hour service fee you have budgeted?"*

Simms: *"I guess, to be accurate, we would have to add this amount to the monthly contract fee we are currently paying."*

Jill: **[Consequences]** *"That means you will have to budget about $27,000 next year in addition to the estimated regular repair service fee?"*

Simms: *"I guess so. I haven't really thought about that being a budgeted item. It really is hidden."*

Jill: **[Criteria]**" So, *one of your criteria for selecting a repair service company is 24-hour, seven days a week service capability so that you could get the repairs when you need them, and that would eliminate the $2,250 per month excess downtime losses. Is that pretty much how you see it?"*

Simms: *"Yes, it looks like that will need to be a minimum requirement."*

Jill: **[Benefit]** *"Are there any other benefits you see in meeting your criteria?"*

Simms: *"It would help the shift supervisors because they wouldn't have to move people around to other lines or account for people not doing anything. It would also lighten their load quite a bit."*

Jill: **[Triggering Events]** *"My next step would be to send you information on how we can meet these criteria. Then, we should set a meeting to explore these and a few related issues. How soon would you like to get together?"*

Simms: *"At $2,250 per month, the sooner, the better."*

Note in some instances, the customer may not know the numbers or may not want to divulge them. Either way, you will want to be prepared with "standards of legitimacy" (discussed in the Effects/Consequences chapter). These are estimates of costs found in similar companies.

P.R.O.S.P.E.C.T. Model Question Sequence

As you read through the book and learn each of the question categories, what might not be readily apparent is that the sequence in which the questions can be asked is less important than the intent of each question being met. Also, note that you could ask all the symptom questions, diagnose several problems, do all the quantification, set criteria, and then ask several benefit questions to the individual or groups of criteria. And finally, go into the Triggering Events questions. Again, it's not the sequence but rather the intent or objective of each question that's important.

Combining Questions

Many of the questions can be combined. You will often find it more natural and comfortable combining questions and reversing their order. Additionally, some early Profile Questions might not get asked until well into the "Triggering Events" Questions. So, for the most part, it is up to you to structure, combine, and sequence the questions so that they are easy, comfortable, and get the information you seek. We will discuss combining questions extensively in the Review module.

2

Profile Questions

Intent

The intent of the Profile Question category is to qualify prospects and identify key buyer influences.

Objectives

- Describe the key characteristics of priority prospects by their market & market segment, by volumes of specified products and services purchased, and by their corporate value system.
- Project current and future customer needs using this profile.
- Qualify and position prospects (according to your business plan) as small, medium, or large accounts and as short or long-term accounts.
- Determine the sales resource allocation based on the account profile.
- Identify the people who make different decisions that influence the sale.
- Summarize the characteristics your most profitable customers have in common.
- Develop questions that will determine the extent to which a current prospect meets the characteristics.

Overview

To determine the questions you would use to qualify a prospect, begin by creating a profile of your most profitable customers by listing the key characteristics they have in common.

With this profile as a template, you can compare how well the prospect matches your most desirable customers. You will be able to determine if a prospect has many of the characteristics by simply looking in a directory or online resource or by asking the prospect.

1. List your current customers by actual sales volume, then assign a shorthand size rating of A, B, or C based on potential volume.
2. Categorize your customers by market and segment in descending order by size rating.
3. Identify the products and services you sell by market, segment, and customer.
4. Identify the customer's critical value systems that influence whom they do business with and how they do business.
5. Identify the people who influence your sales by the types of decisions they make.
6. Summarize the firmographic, demographic, and psychographic (values) characteristics your most profitable customers have in common, then develop questions that will determine the extent to which a current prospect meets the characteristics. Finally, resources other than decision-makers can be used to find this information.

Profile by Potential Sales Volume

There are several ways to begin to profile your prospects. The best way is to list your current customers in order by the potential volume of purchases they could make from you. The volume identifier could be gross dollars or units.

Generally, salespeople rank their prospects and customers by size using letters:

- A for large
- B for medium
- C for small

These A, B, and C categories are not the only ones. For very large volumes, you can add AAA or AA. For smaller companies, use the D classification.

Remember, the sizes are relative to the account potential the company represents. These letter designations enable you to make judgment calls concerning the time, money, and other resources you want to dedicate to obtain, grow, and retain the account.

Many companies in business-to-business (B2B) selling will derive the best results from the "B" size accounts. Of course, this does not mean that you should overlook others.

The next step in qualifying is determining your present accounts' sales and buying cycles.

Sales and Buying Cycles

The ***"sales cycle"*** is measured by the average time it takes to "sell" an account by size categories. For example:

- A + size accounts may take 1 to 5 years
- A-size accounts may take 12 to 24 months
- B-size accounts may take 6 to 12 months
- C-size accounts may take 3 to 6 months
- D-size accounts may take less than 3 months

In general, the larger the company, the more formal and rigid the purchasing policies will be, the more decision-makers involved, and consequently, the longer it will take.

The ***"buying cycle"*** is the frequency and procedure in which a customer buys your product or service. For example, it may only take one day to convince the customer to purchase from you, but the current contract with a competitor still has two years left on it. Or your service will have to wait until the next fiscal year's budget is approved.

Areas to Profile by Size

Customer
Volume
Sales Cycle
Buying Cycle
Size

Some examples:

Customer: Hops Along
Volume: 100,000
Sales Cycle: 1 year
Buying Cycle: 1-year contract
Size: A

Customer: Jones Soda
Volume: 50,000
Sales Cycle: 9 months
Buying Cycle: 1-year contract
Size: B

Customer: Martin & Seams
Volume: 25,000
Sales Cycle: 3 months
Buying Cycle: 3 months
Size: C

Customer: The Light Company

Volume: 250,000
Sales Cycle: 6 months
Buying Cycle: 3-year contract
Size: A

Customer: Plastic Bits LLC
Volume: 50,000
Sales Cycle: 3 months
Buying Cycle: No contract (30-day notice)
Size: B

Customer: Widgets R Us
Volume: 15,000
Sales Cycle: 1 month
Buying Cycle: 3 months
Size: C

Customer: Community Hospital
Volume: 75,000
Sales Cycle: 1 year
Buying Cycle: 1-year contract
Size: B

Your Customers

On a sheet of paper, list a sampling of your actual customers by size.

Profile Customers by Markets and Market Segments

A "market" is a group of businesses or individuals that have identifiable characteristics in common. Often a market is defined as an industry category such as medical, service, manufacturing, or utilities. A market could also be defined as a group of people categorized by values, ages, or occupations. For example, yuppies, managers, or gray markets.

A "market segment" is a narrowing or further refinement of the definition of a market. For example, the manufacturing market has multiple segments such as electronics, medical, printing, computer, and so on. They are all manufacturers but of different items.

Begin by looking at the customer list you completed on the previous page, and this time, categorize them by their market and market segment.

How you classify your customers is only important to the extent that you can use your classification to locate others in the same market segments. This will help clarify where you could find other potential customers and the specific types of products/services you might sell to them.

Identify **indicators** that suggest a need for your Unique Selling Points (USPs).

For example, Jill Ryan's company provides services 24 hours a day, seven days a week. She would look for companies operating on the same schedule, especially when competing against other service providers who only offer services during the regular 8 to 5 business days. If the customers use a wet gray (increases need) or don't have specialist maintenance personnel for the equipment, they would need to pre-diagnose over the phone to ensure they have the right parts for the repair.

As you uncover more of your Unique Selling Points (USPs) in the next module, you can use them to help qualify your prospects.

Building on the earlier examples:

Customer: Hops Along

Volume: 100,000

Sales Cycle: 1 year

Buying Cycle: 1-year contract

Size: A

Market: Food

Market Segment: Brewing

USP Need: Wet wash down

Customer: Jones Soda
Volume: 50,000
Sales Cycle: 9 months
Buying Cycle: 1-year contract
Size: B
Market: Food
Market Segment: Soft drinks
USP Need: Wet wash down

Customer: Martin & Seams
Volume: 25,000
Sales Cycle: 3 months
Buying Cycle: 3 months
Size: C
Market: Food
Market Segment: Packaged snacks
USP Need: Operating 24/7

Customer: The Light Company
Volume: 250,000
Sales Cycle: 6 months
Buying Cycle: 3-year contract
Size: A
Market: Utility
Market Segment: Electric
USP Need: Operating 24/7

Customer: Plastic Bits LLC
Volume: 50,000
Sales Cycle: 3 months
Buying Cycle: No contract (30-day notice)

Size: B
Market: Manufacturing
Market Segment:
USP Need: Previsit Diagnostic

Customer: Widgets R Us
Volume: 15,000
Sales Cycle: 1 month
Buying Cycle: 3 months
Size: C
Market: Manufacturing
Market Segment: Hardware
USP Need: Pre-visit Diagnostic

Customer: Community Hospital
Volume: 75,000
Sales Cycle: 1 year
Buying Cycle: 1-year contract
Size: B
Market: Medical
Market Segment: Hospital Food Service
USP Need: Wet wash down

Your Markets and Market Segments

List your customers by the markets and market segments you would categorize them under. List them in descending order of size.

TIP: If you use your company's complete customer list, you may uncover customers in markets and market segments that have not been fully developed. Don't discount them. Further exploration of these markets could lead to a tremendous boost in sales. This is particularly important if your current markets are not growing.

More than one company has made a complete market shift due to this type of exploration, and more than one company has developed entirely new product lines and new services for these markets.

Customer:
  Volume:
  Sales Cycle:
  Buying Cycle:
  Size:
  Market:
  Market Segment:
  USP Need:

Profile Customers by Market Segments and Your Products/Services

In this step, you'll discover what your customers buy (and not buy) from you. It will also show what a prospective customer in a similar market segment and size category might potentially purchase.

You complete this step by first building a spreadsheet-style grid. At the top of the page, identify the market and market segment this list will cover. Then, down the left-hand side of the page, list your customers in this market segment, sequenced from large to small. Across the top of the page, list your products and services — next, review each customer to identify what and how much they buy.

This step in the Profiling process provides an additional refinement to the "size" or volume category by defining what goes into making up that number. In this example, "units" could represent units of service or the number of products or dollars per category. In this example, we'll use a company with three core products (or categories of products).

Market Segment: Manufacturing – Printing
  Customer: Big Co. Inc.

Size: A
Product 1: 2200 units
Product 2: None
Product 3: 1000 units

Customer: Large Co. Inc
Size: A
Product 1: 1800 units
Product 2: 1200 units
Product 3: 800 units

Customer: Mid Co. Inc.
Size: B
Product 1: 700 units
Product 2: 500 units
Product 3: 300 units

Customer: NewCo. LLC
Size: B
Product 1: None
Product 2: 300 units
Product 3: None

Your Customers by Products/Services Purchased

Identify and write the market segment in the box in the heading below. Next, list your actual customers in descending order of size. Across the top of the form, list your products/services by actual items or by categories of products/services.

Look for Patterns

What are similar size accounts buying by volume and type of products and services? Are there any noticeable gaps that need further exploration?

Ask yourself, is this 100% of the available business? If they are not buying a particular product or service, why not? It could be simply that there is no need. However, if other customers of the same size and in the same category are buying that product or service, then look again.

With this information, we can now ask prospects questions about the types of products/services they purchase and know the potential volume.

Cross-selling is one of the best strategies to improve your sales results rapidly and dramatically!

Customer:

Size:

Product 1:

Product 2:

Product 3:

Customer:

Size:

Product 1:

Product 2:

Product 3:

Customer:

Size:

Product 1:

Product 2:

Product 3:

Profile Value Systems

Identify your customers' value systems. Value is the measure of desire for something. It is the strength of emotional attachment. If you value a more formal corporate dress uniform, you will be attracted to other people with the same or similar values.

If you value community involvement, you will be attracted to other people with a similar value and tend to move away from people without that value.

When your company's values match the prospect's, a natural attraction occurs, and your ability to sell increases, you gain a competitive edge.

Some of the values listed below could be important to what you sell. Determine which are important and think about clues that suggest that the person or company has that value.

Values: Innovative or conservative

Clues: *Does the company use high-tech equipment, i.e., computers, E-mail? How does the staff dress? Does the company encourage continuous improvement, or is the attitude "If it ain't broke, don't fix it." What is the office decorum? How do people in the company talk about innovation?*

Values: Innovative or conservative

Clues: *Does the company invest in training or just buy the equipment and let the employees figure out how to use it? What is the office or plant atmosphere?*

Values: Value-driven or price-driven

Clues: *Do the people look at the overall impact on the organization or just on their department? Does the company buy the cheapest items available or base their purchases on return on investment?*

Corporate Values Important to Your Sale

Identify the top three values important to what you sell, then define the clues that suggest the person or company has the value.

Profile the Decision Makers

In all sales, different decision-making roles influence the sale. One person may fill several roles, or several people may be in each role. Each of them is a decision-maker, but they decide about different aspects of the purchase. It is important to know who plays each role in your sale so that you can ensure that the ten buyer beliefs are targeted to their area of decision-making authority and established with each of them.

Decision Maker Roles

In every sale, different types of decisions are made. Sometimes, one person makes all the decisions; at other times, several people can cluster together to make one type of decision. One person could play many decision-making roles, or many people could be playing one role.

The roles and types of decisions we'll focus on include:

- **Final Authority $:** Controls the budgets you impact. Interested in Return on Investment, Rate of Return, or Return on Assets.
- **Specifier $:** Sets functional performance criteria. Interested in performance & cost justification
- **Negotiator $:** Focus on getting the best terms and conditions. Is interested in high feature to low price ratio. Favorable Terms and Conditions.
- **End-User:** Plan of action and involvement in implementation. Interested in your credibility, user-friendliness, and input in areas affecting them
- **Coach / Ally:** Guide you through the buying process. Interested in your credibility
- **Recommender:** Third-party, "unbiased" reference. Interested in their reputation for being helpful with credible resources.

If it's one or two people playing the various roles, you can tell which role they're in by the types of questions they ask. By knowing about the different roles, you can begin to focus and structure your answers to the kind of decision needed.

For example, asking a person (spouse or corporate executive) how they made their last decision to buy a _______ will provide you with valuable information about the process they use and who plays what role. The person giving you the information is in the "Coach" role.

Just remember that all these types of decisions must be made before the purchase will be made. Help the buyers by asking the kinds of questions and information that will support the decision you would like to see made.

Notice that three decision-makers are interested in the money but in different ways. And three of the decision-makers have an interest in your credibility.

Let's take a more detailed look at each role and the types of decisions they represent.

Final Authority ($)

The Final Authority is the person who:

- pays attention to Return on Investment (ROI), Rate of Return, and Return on Assets
- has control over all the budgets this purchase will impact
- can move money from one budget to another

The Final Authority controls the budgets impacted by your products and services. Suppose your products and services affect two departments. In that case, you must find the person to whom these two department managers report to find the person with budgetary responsibility for both departments.

Managers usually have specific limits on their spending authority. This means that the larger the dollar value, the higher in the organization you must search to find the actual final authority. The final authority is primarily interested in R.O.I. So, when you meet with this person, talk about the Return on Investment (ROI), how much they will get in return for buying from you, and the Rate of Return (ROR) or how fast that return will come.

Another measure important to many is the Return on Assets. This measure shows how good management is at generating profits from its assets (divide net income by total assets). This may be a good measure of what you sell. Use its revenue-generating capacity divided by the cost to get the results. Include the ROR calculation as well.

Remember, just because someone has the authority to purchase from you, i.e., purchasing departments, does not mean they are the Final Authority. By our definition, the Final Authority is responsible for the budgets impacted by your products/services. Unless the purchasing department buys for their department, they will rarely be the actual Final Authority.

Remember, the Final Authority is the person who can decide to re-allocate money. S/he has the power of the pen. S/he is over the budgets you impact and can move money from one to the other to maximize the benefits to all areas or departments of responsibility.

The size of the company, the size of the purchase price, the importance of your offering to the company's success, and the number of areas you will impact determine your Final Authority.

With this definition, you may not need to call on the CEO of a company; rather, the appropriate level decision-maker may be anyone from the office manager to a department head to the board of directors.

To find the Final Authority, draw an organizational chart that includes the areas or departments you will impact the most and determine who is responsible for those areas. You may want to look at the percent impact you have in each area to identify the most important people you will need to convince to support you on your way to connecting with the Final Authority.

Specifier ($)

The Specifier is a person who is interested in:

- performance specifications and capabilities
- cost justification
- unique advantages in how they deliver the benefits better than competing ways
- unique benefits that increase the functional value of the product or service

The Specifier sets the product and service performance criteria. They also set selection criteria based on "how" the products and services will be delivered and other supplier requirements.

Usually, this person is a functional area manager or supervisor who has first-hand knowledge of the value of your products and services but may not have the *final* power of the pen. Specifiers are often found by determining who controls functional performance specifications for your products and services. Usually, there is more than one person in this role.

Specifiers can also be consultants the customer hires to define the project and select suppliers. Consultants can also be "Recommenders" (see below) based on their role.

The key benefit that Specifiers want is the peace of mind that the product or service will meet their requirements and decision-making criteria.

Specifiers are also very interested in "cost justification." Remember, they have to get their purchases approved at a higher level. If you do not help them cost-justify the expenditure and they cannot do it on their own, then the probability that they will attempt to get approval decreases dramatically, and the sale will stall.

For example, if you sell machine tools, engineering, shop supervisor, and others rewarded based on performance would meet this definition. They may have budgets for what you sell. Still, if your price is higher than the competitors or outside the limits of the Specifier's budget, then you will need to use the Specifier's facts and figures to establish the value of your products or services. You would define this value in terms of what you can save the customer or how much additional production you can provide that will add to the productivity and profit of the output. The bottom line for the Specifiers is their ability to answer the question, *"How can you cost-justify spending this much?"*

For example, if your service is available 24 hours a day, the customer operates 24 hours a day, and the competitor is only available for 8 hours. Some capabilities you can offer may be helpful to the customer when you are available, but your competitor is not. If none come to mind, you may not need to operate 24 hours a day, or you might consider developing some to give you a competitive advantage.

Take a close look at your capabilities and the advantages and benefits they provide to select those most appropriate for those in the Specifier role.

Negotiator ($)

The Negotiator is the person who is interested in the following:

- getting the lowest price for the greatest number of features

- getting the best terms for delivery and warranty
- wants the greatest number of features for the least amount of money

Negotiators want the best terms, including pricing, delivery, and warranty. They focus on the "price/feature" ratio: the more features, the more they are willing to spend.

During negotiations, list every possible feature that would have a remote possibility of being used. Whenever you are asked to lower your price, be sure that you take out features of equal value. Never give in to pressure, only principle. Cost justification for each feature must be done before you negotiate. You cannot negotiate unless you know the value of what you are negotiating from the customer's perspective.

Negotiators are often found in purchasing departments. However, the functional area manager will frequently negotiate and then submit the requisition to the Purchasing Department to complete the purchase order and other paperwork as necessary.

Adversarial-style negotiators want you to see your offering as a "line-item" commodity, even if it's not. Your job is to point out and establish the value of the differences in the product, if any, and the differences related to how you and your company do business. Look at the additional capabilities you bring to the table, including anything from training to having the products in stock, shipping, and ease of doing business with you and your company.

NOTICE that the three previous decision-makers (types of decisions) were interested in the money ($), but each wanted to discuss it differently than the other two.

End-User (Credibility & User Friendliness)

The End User is a person who will:

- use the product/service
- benefit from its use
- want to know if this will make their job easier or harder

The End Users or consumers are the people who will actually use your products and services or activate their use, i.e., call for delivery. End Users have developed a comfort zone of familiarity with what they are currently using, so resistance to change must be factored into building a user-friendly plan for implementation, or you risk having your sales sabotaged.

"How easy is doing business with you and your company?" "What steps are necessary to change your products and services?" "How well do they work compared to what I'm currently doing?" "How easy is it to get support?"

Remember that End Users may not be able to say "yes," but they can often say "no." And even if the company buys it anyway, they may not use or misuse it. In either case, the supplier frequently loses out on future business.

Coach (Credibility)

A Coach is a person who is willing to:

- guide you through the buying process
- identify decision-makers
- advise you on how to make a good impression

The coach is anyone inside the buying loop who can and is willing to guide you through the buying maze. They can help point out other decision-makers, tell you what's most important to them, and advise you on what not to do.

Your objective is to turn all the decision-makers you interact with into your coach.

The quickest and easiest way to do this is with the magic question, "Could you help me, please?" Very few people will turn down that request, would you?

Focus on what they are interested in - credibility. By helping you, they look good.

Related coach roles include:

Sponsor: This person will help you get the meetings but won't make decisions that are rightfully their subordinates to make. They are usually found in management positions.

Mentor: They will guide you through the buying process and be willing to run some limited interference for you. They like what you bring to the table in terms of products and service and in terms of style, integrity, and other qualities they appreciate.

To discover your most probable initial Coaches, ask yourself whom you would contact if you heard something was happening with a competitor in one of your accounts. Who would be the first person you would call to get the scoop on what's happening? Try this with several accounts of the same size and industry. If the same or similar position title comes up repeatedly, you know who you want to call to get to know early on in your prospect accounts.

Recommender (Credibility)

The Recommender is the person who:

- is outside of the buying loop
- acts as a "third party" reference
- appears unbiased
- can, as a consultant, act as a Specifier

Recommenders are usually outside the buying loop. They are your third-party references, customer lists, and referral sources, even consultants hired by the company to make recommendations. If you don't provide these references, the decision-makers will seek out their own.

The unfortunate part is that they may not know your good customers and may ask someone very satisfied with one of your competitors. Recommenders are primarily concerned about their reputation and how they will be represented to others.

Multiple People, Multiple Roles: We stated earlier that one person could play more than one role, or you could have a situation where more than one person is in a role. You can tell which role a person is in by the types of questions they ask.

Money: Notice that the Final Authority, the Specifier, and the Negotiator are all interested in money but from a different point of view.

Credibility: Three decision-making roles (End User, Coach, and Recommender) are primarily interested in credibility. No one wants to hear the boss scream, "Who brought those bozos in here?"

User Friendliness: People have too much to contend with daily that a steep learning curve to use your product or service, to figure out how to buy your product, or to try to maintain it will be rejected in favor of the easy-to-buy, use, and maintain.

Get in their Heads: For each of the decision-makers, try to view your product and service from their perspective on how they will get and use it. Learn their concerns and approach your answers from that perspective.

Example Profile Questions

- Who needs it? (name specific market segments)
- Where are they located? (Territory)
- What is our optimal level of efficiency? (name the volume that is most cost-effective for you to produce and deliver, i.e., hours of service, units of product)
- What size company could use that volume? (A, B, C)
- What size correlation is easiest to determine? (number of employees, annual gross revenues, square footage of space, etc., equate to the volume of purchases made for a specific product or service)
- How long does it take to get that type or size customer? (sales cycle)
- How do they buy? (buying cycle, i.e., annually, quarterly, or as needed)
- What values influence my ability to obtain, maintain, and grow the account?
- What special needs can I fill with my Unique Selling Points?
- Who are the decision-makers?
- What list, directory, or online resource can I use to identify them?

Business-to-Business Example

Product/Service: Motor Control Repair
Market: Manufacturing
Segment: Food Processing

Profile Characteristics:

- Located in Texas
- 10 to 20 conveyor systems per facility (correlated ratio - 25 employees/system)
- Conveyor motor controllers are out of warranty (1 year)
- 24/7 operation
- Use annual contracts
- Value-based decisions

Qualifying Questions

- Where are you located?
- How many conveyor systems do you have at this facility?
- How old are your motor controllers?
- What are your hours of production?
- What is the length of time for repair service agreements?
- Do you want the lowest price or lowest bottom line for the company?

Source of information

- Directories, Internet
- Coaches or anyone in the company familiar with operations (directory)
- Purchasing, operations people, maintenance personnel
- Anyone familiar with operations
- Purchasing
- V-P Operations, V-P Finance, Purchasing

Decision Makers

- **Final Authority**: Vice-President of Operations
- **Specifier:** Operations Manager, Maintenance Manager
- **Coach/Mentor/Sponsor:** Night Shift Supervisor, Maintenance Manager
- **Negotiator:** Purchasing Agent, V-P Finance
- **End-User:** Shift Supervisors, Maintenance Supervisors
- **Recommender:** BESCO Foods and Chickens, LTD

Construct Your Profile

Use the form on the next page to build a profile for one of your specific products/services, market, and market segments. Recognize you will need to make this type of profile for each of your products/services for each market segment.

Steps to Follow:

- Identify a specific product or service.
- Identify the market and market segment for the product/service.
- List your most desirable customer characteristics and value systems in the first column.
- Write out the question you will ask to determine the extent to which the prospect's answer matches yours (characteristics).
- Identify the source(s) you will use to get the answers.
- Identify, by the usual title, the decision-makers involved in your sale for this size company.

Finding Pre-Qualified Prospects

Having a list of contactable leads that match the profile of your most desirable customers ranks right up there at the top of what you need to be successful.

So, now that you know what a qualified prospect looks like, you need to find resources that will provide you with what could be considered a pre-qualified list of potential prospects.

Here are some specific resources to build your lists and get the answers to some of your profile questions so you can quickly qualify your prospects.

Personal Lists

What organizations do you belong to? Get to know the other members. You may find that in your network, you know people who will become customers or could refer you to people who could become your customers.

Newspapers

Read the local newspaper and Business Journal for job promotions and transfers. Watch for business announcements such as new offices, relocation, etc. Many of your prospective customers will appear here.

Chamber of Commerce

Try the local Chamber of Commerce. Helping to grow a local business (including yours) is part of their charter. Often, they will publish a directory of business, industry, trade, and professional organizations.

Associations

Associations are fertile ground for prospects. Look for a directory of professional, trade, and business associations or organizations in your market niche or territory. Association trade shows, where your prospects exhibit, are also a prime source of high-quality prospects and referral sources.

The Internet

The volume of information on a keyword search can be overwhelming. Not all of the information will meet your needs. That means you'll need to learn advanced search techniques to keep the volume of information manageable and on target.

Social Media

LinkedIn, Alignable, and others are business-oriented resources with an enormous capacity to help find and make contact.

List Brokers

Commercial assistance is available through various mailing list companies. A list broker company can provide you with lists of targeted decision-makers to contact. Fees can range from $40 per thousand names with contact information to $1.25 each. They can also help you build a custom list to meet any characteristics you want to use.

Summary

Summarize the common characteristics you've identified to construct a profile of your most desirable (valued) customers. This profile or template can then be used to develop a series of questions that will quickly and effectively qualify new prospects.

In looking at our clients' lost sales, I noted that many were because they had not fully qualified the prospects.

First, the sellers did not know who the decision-makers were, and they didn't have sufficient time to build the level of trust and rapport necessary to conduct the sales interview with the ones they did know.

Second, the seller discovered the sales opportunity when the Request for Proposal arrived on the desk. That left no time for the sales process, no time or ability to interview the key decision-makers, and no opportunity to do a cost-benefit analysis comparing capabilities. Those responsible for responding to the RFIs, RFPs, and RFQs were not trained on how to pick up the sales process going forward from this point.

Third, a mismatch in their corporate "value" systems was the root cause. As you might have expected, the customer wanted cheap, and the seller focused on premium quality level pricing with a more significant bottom-line impact, but the initial price was not acceptable. Without the opportunity to do the proper due diligence found in the research step of this sales model, this was not discovered until too late in the process. Using the P.R.O.S.P.E.C.T. Model helped increase the number of qualified prospects. It also helped prevent price pressure by quantifying value going directly to the bottom line with the decision-makers that mattered.

So, as you can see, you may initially pre-qualify a prospect, but if you find that there isn't enough time, access, or information to do your sales job, then you might want to downgrade them from being qualified to maybe the "suspect" level.

3

Research Questions

Intent

The intent of the Research Questions category is to gain customer and competitor information and develop a win/win strategy.

Objectives

- Gain an in-depth understanding of your customer's business, particularly in the areas of:
- their products and services and how what you sell can impact them
- the critical processes necessary for them to have, and how what you sell impacts this process
- their business plan as it relates to the products and services you sell
- their selling environment and marketplace
- Identify current suppliers and the products/services they sell to this customer.
- Develop a win/win sales strategy based on customer needs, competitor's weaknesses, and your strengths.

This question category is divided into two sections:

- This first section is designed to help you understand your prospective customer's business and which critical needs will most likely be neglected by your competitor.
- The second section is designed to help you understand critical information regarding your competitors.

Overview

Now that we know we are dealing with a qualified prospect, we can move on to learn more about their specific business operations that we can impact with our products/services and how we deliver them.

All businesses have four needs or objectives:

1. Increase their ability to generate revenues.
2. Reduce operating costs.
3. Strengthen or enhance their image.
4. Lessen vulnerability in the marketplace.

To help our customers meet these business objectives, we must learn about:

- prospect's **products/services** that you can impact with your strengths
- **critical processes** they use to produce the products/services they sell, and how your products/services can improve their process and outcomes related to one or more of the four business needs
- customer's **business plan** specifically as it relates to your products/services
- **current and competing suppliers** and their areas of weakness, where you have strengths, where the customer has needs

Distinction Between Profile and Research Questions

Research Questions can sometimes look like Profile Questions. For example, "What volume are you currently ordering?" This question could be a Profile Question in one case and a Research Question in another.

To distinguish between the two, you would look at the "intent" of the question. If the answer would qualify or disqualify the prospect, then it is a Profile Question. If, however, the answer to the question will help build a package of products/services to be introduced as a part of your sales strategy, then the question's intent would make it a Research Question.

However, in the end, it doesn't matter if you call it a Profile or a Research Question. What does matter is the information you get. If the answer to the question qualifies or disqualifies, you must get to it as quickly as possible. If it helps build your business case, you've got more time.

Understanding the Prospect's Business

Your research into a company should be designed to discover how your Unique Selling Points can help the prospect meet their business needs better than the competitors can. When you do this, you uncover their needs for your Unique Selling Points.

Understand their businesses in these three areas:

1. Products and services
2. Critical processes
3. Business plan
4. Current and Competing Suppliers

Prospect's products/services

Understand how what you sell can make the prospect's products/services better than the competitor can. Apply your Unique Selling Points to discover ways you can make their products and services better than their competitors.

To investigate the prospect's products/services, you may want to use their materials such as:

- product literature
- corporate image brochures
- website

Information provided by internal interviews and non-competitive suppliers is also valuable. You should have this information before you interview for critical processes. You can fill in voids about the products/services as you ask about the processes.

Questions to Ask:

- *What do your customers look for in your product or service?*
- *Where or how in your product/service do you use what we sell?*
- *How does that impact what you sell?*
- *How can we make what we sell easier for you to sell?*
- *How would your customers respond to having _____ (USP)?*

Make a note of the questions you might ask in this area. Tie at least one of them to your USPs.

Prospect's critical processes

Two things to understand about your customers are how they make their money and how you and your products can impact them positively to meet their business needs.

Look at the workflow your product/service would affect to find areas where you can make a measurable difference.

During your interviews, in person or on the phone, ask the prospects about their basic workflows and the company's goals. Then, you can explore how things would improve if your products were being used and your Unique Selling Points applied.

Questions to Ask:

- *Could you briefly walk me through the process you use for your production line?*
- *How do you currently _______?*
- *Where are the bottlenecks that cause slow production?*
- *Who do you use as the supplier for this portion of the process?*
- *How would that impact the flow if you could apply _____ (USP)?*

Make a note of the questions you might ask in this area. Tie at least one of them to your USPs.

Prospect's business plan

You want to know a little about your prospect's business plan, so you know about events that could affect the company's ability to buy from you. You don't want to begin the sales process only to learn they will reorganize and no longer use your service.

Additionally, if you're selling to the leadership team, recognize that they invest in those products and services that will help them complete their strategic initiatives. Mid-management has MBOs (management by objective) that usually align with specific relevant strategic initiatives. So, it pays to know their goals and plans to determine how you can help the prospect achieve those goals.

Some issues you should research are:

- *Can you briefly describe your company's plans related to ___ for next year? Long-term?*
- *What strategic initiatives are given top priority?*
- *What MBOs are priorities in these areas?*
- *What kind of buying cycle occurs for your manufacturing processes?*
- *Where do you see your growth coming from in the next few years?*
- *Will you be expanding in this area?*

- *Is this a regularly budgeted product and service?*
- *How frequently do you purchase this product/service?*
- *Do you use long-term supplier agreements?*
- *Do you plan any major changes in budgeting this next fiscal year?*
- *Are there any proposed changes to the organizational structure that I should be aware of that might impact our ability to help you achieve your goals?*

Sources for this information include:

- Annual and Quarterly reports
- Industry Publications
- Customer suppliers (non-competitive)
- Internal interviews
- Internet

Make a note of the questions you might ask in this area. Tie at least one of them to your USPs.

Understanding Competitors

To complete the sales strategy development process, we must research our competitors to see which needs they can fill, which needs they cannot, and which needs we can fill better. We do this by completing a competitor analysis.

In sports, on the battlefield, or in sales, we must know who and what we're up against. To "compete" by definition means we have a competitor (even if it's "do nothing"). Professional sports coaches would not last long if they did not develop a strategy that would neutralize the competitor's strong points and focus on playing the game in areas where the competitor is weak, and they are strong.

Three Common Types of Competitor Analysis

There are three common types of competitor analysis:

- Business
- Marketing
- Sales

Business Competitor Analysis

The primary purpose of Business Competitor Analysis is to provide management with information about high-level topics concerning competitors. This includes corporate strategies, product introductions, partnerships, and ownership changes. A common form of this type of competitor analysis is the SWOT Analysis (internal Strengths and Weaknesses and external Opportunities and Threats).

Marketing Competitor Analysis

Marketing style Competitor Analysis focuses on highlighting your strengths to fulfill your offering's primary purpose. When put into a "competitive comparison closing strategy format, they can help offset the competitor's strengths.

Sales Competitor Analysis

This style of competitor analysis developed by Sales Training International first identifies areas where the competitor is strong. This is where your objections come from when up against this competitor. Once you know the strengths, you'll want to find a way to neutralize them directly (offer the same or similar capability) or "offset" them with benefits you can offer (your strengths) that the competitor cannot.

Next, this analysis looks at the competitor's weaknesses, where you have corresponding strengths. These corresponding strengths will be used to influence the buying specifications and offset the competitors' strengths, where you cannot neutralize them directly.

The primary purpose of Sales Competitor Analysis is to provide information necessary to:

- Develop a sales strategy to neutralize business reasons for staying with a competitor
- Identify where to focus the sales interview for quickly uncovering needs only you can fill
- Identify where and how to measure value
- Set specifications to get the prospect to rule out the competition
- Create objections for the competitor

Competitor to Product/Service Matrix

Begin by making a list of competitors down the left side of a sheet of paper. Across the top of the sheet, list your products/services. Where you compete with a competitor's product/service, put a check mark, and you'll want to conduct a competitor analysis.

Under normal conditions, at most, you'll compete with 3 to 5 competitors or categories of competitors.

Developing Your Competitor Analysis

In this Competitor Analysis, there are two sets of counterbalancing areas of information:

The first contains the customer's perceived competitor's advantages, countered by how you neutralize or offset each advantage.

The second contains the Competitor's Weaknesses stacked up against your strengths in those areas.

Note that the layout for the Competitor Analysis is best displayed in a box divided into four quadrants.

- The **upper left quadrant** would contain the Customer Perceived Competitor's Advantages.

- The **upper right quadrant** would contain how your company neutralizes or offsets the competitor's advantages. You do this on a one-to-one basis for each of their Advantages.
- The **lower left quadrant** would contain the competitor's weaknesses.
- The **lower right quadrant** would contain your company's strengths. Again, this is done on a one-to-one basis where you identify a strength for each of their weaknesses. These become your Unique Selling Points (USPs).

Customer Perceived Competitor's Advantages (upper left quadrant): Why do your prospects buy from them? What does the competitor consistently point out in their sales presentations, advertisements, and literature? Listen carefully when you ask someone (but never a prospect) to tell you what they know about a competitor. These are often the reasons people buy from them.

These **perceived advantages are the source of the competitor-based objections you get**, spoken or unspoken. This is what the prospect knows about. If the prospect feels the advantage is important and you don't have it, they will object. By gathering and recording the competitor's perceived strengths and advantages, you will know what objections to expect from the prospect when you are up against this competitor.

Your Neutralizing Benefits (upper right quadrant): How do you neutralize each of their advantages? If you are both "large" companies, then it's a wash. However, if they use it in their sales literature or presentation, we recommend you do the same to neutralize its ability to create an objection.

If they have strengths you can't directly neutralize with something equal or better, you'll need to reach down in the lower right-hand quadrant to find offsetting capabilities where you're strong, and your competitor is weak. These become the trade-off capabilities you can offer to offset competitor strengths you can't provide.

Competitor's Weaknesses (lower left quadrant): First, look at the product or service you have selected for any weakness they may have. One way to do this is to look at your strengths, record them in the appropriate box, and record a corresponding weakness in the "competitor's weakness" box. Next, look at the competitor's company. All companies have weaknesses. Dig hard and deep. There is some difference in how they deliver their products and services from how your company provides them. Find them.

Your Strengths (lower right quadrant): First, counter each of your competitor's known weaknesses with your area of strength. Next, look at any strengths you have that are not listed and list them. Then, go back into the competitor's weakness box and record the corresponding weakness. You might want to validate the weakness by reviewing their website's information, talking to colleagues, and accessing other resources.

This section is critical. This section is where you discover and clarify your Unique Selling Points (USP) in this sales opportunity, which you will learn to set as Criteria for selecting a supplier. Without these (USP), you will not be able to establish the value of your solutions to be greater than that of your competitor. This is the heart of your sales strategy. Take your time with this.

Sources for information to complete the Competitor Analysis come from your competitor's literature (print and online), interactions with strong coaches or allies in customer organizations, other sales and marketing professionals, research and development staff, and others.

Case Study: The "Jill Ryan" Scenario

During the Introduction chapter of this book, you saw an example of the P.R.O.S.P.E.C.T. Model in action using Jill Ryan's motor controller repair service. Really, it could be anything because, as you'll note, we're not using her service; instead, we are considering it a commodity, so we can explore how her company delivers the service and how they do business as the primary way in which the quantifiable differentiate themselves in their highly competitive market.

This case study was also used earlier during the introduction to value selling and to demonstrate how to develop the Profile Questions. It will be used throughout the remainder of the book to provide examples of each of the question categories.

Recall that Jill Ryan sells a repair service for electronic motor control systems. These systems control motor speed based on the load and demand of the conveyor. Her service is considered a commodity because, on the surface, there do not appear to be any significant differences between what she offers and what her competitors offer, except for the price.

The Profile of her most desirable customers include:

1. Are in manufacturing, food processing, or distribution industries
2. Use multiple (10 to 20) individually controlled conveyor systems
3. Run 24-hour, 7-day operations
4. Facilities are not climate-controlled or have wet wash downs of the equipment.
5. Motor controllers are out of warranty
6. The Final Authority is the Vice-President of Operations

Research the Prospect's Products and Services: Jill found out that the company she has targeted does its routine maintenance but contracts for motor controller repair service.

Neither the company nor its customers store much of the product due to refrigeration costs. The customers want "just-in-time" (J.I.T.) delivery. This means that the company must process continuously and ship immediately. Downtime could mean shipments are not being made and customers are running out of a product.

Research the Prospect's Critical Processes: As a food processor, they use numerous wet wash downs, putting extra strain on the controllers. If a conveyor goes down, the crew goes home until it's back up and running. This hits morale, which impacts productivity.

Research the Prospect's Business Plan: The conveyor systems are aging, and the company has no plans to replace them. This means repair work will continue to increase.

Competitor Analysis: Jill faces two competitors in her territory that offer the same service for a much lower price. Her company charges $125 per service hour, while her competitors only charge $80 per service hour. As a budgeted line item - "contract repair service," Jill must keep her competitor analyses updated. Her competitor for this sale is Hardware Inc.

Without using graphics, the competitor's "low price" advantage is offset by Jill's "low bottom-line impact." The competitor's "Experienced Technicians" are offset by Jill's "Certified Technicians," and so on.

Customer Perceived Competitor's Advantages

1. Lower Price
2. Experienced technicians
3. In business, many years and has great customer relationships

For each Advantage, Jill must provide a way to neutralize it or risk it becoming an objection.

Jill's Company: Neutralizing or Offsetting Benefits

1. Low bottom-line impact
2. Certified technicians
3. New company with fresh ideas on how to provide better service to the customer

Next, Jill will identify each competitor's weaknesses where she has corresponding strengths **in this sales opportunity**. Again, each competitor's weaknesses are matched with one of Jill's strengths on a one-to-one basis.

Competitor's Weaknesses

1. Business hours are 7 AM to 6 PM - 5 days
2. Usually, they have to return to their shop to get parts
3. Technicians not certified by specialized training and test

Jill's company: Strengths

1. 24-hour, 7-day service availability.
2. Troubleshoot on the phone before going to the customer's location - have the right parts.
3. Factory-certified technicians.

Include Company Differentiation

It is important to note that the strengths Jill focuses on are not directly related to the service itself but rather to how her company delivers the service.

If you have products/services that can be differentiated based on performance and other attributes, use them and then continue to differentiate based on how your company does business.

Differentiating Factors

The following list is intended to help stimulate thinking to identify some of the less obvious factors you might use to differentiate your company and products from the competition. This list was developed over the years working with companies that sold pure commodities. These can be added to the list of Unique Selling Points.

Remember that you, as a customer, want to know from your suppliers how they can deliver what the competitors can. Then, you want to understand how each supplier's capabilities differ and how those differences affect you, good or bad!

Company: Organizational infrastructure, plans, emphasis, i.e., quality, team, planning, financial stability, communications, corporate integrity, interdepartmental knowledge, reputation, experience in the industry, Internet presence, e-commerce capabilities, track records, i.e., safety, environmental

Personnel: Training, commitment, capabilities, special skills/departments, experience in the industry, quality of staff, accessibility, turnover that impacts relationships

Facilities: Location, number, redundancies/backup, modernization, capabilities, inventory size, accessibility

Materials: Feed stock quality, source/availability, procurement processes, uniform product

Manufacturing: Product line - breadth/depth, product superiority, reliability engineering, lead time requirements, unique or proprietary manufacturing processes, percent contaminants, product consistency, quality assurance/-controls, safety and environmental record, custom capabilities, flexibility, real-time order status monitoring, outsourcing, short notice changes, special size orders capabilities

Distribution: Distribution system, packaging, shipping/transporting, tracking/monitoring, inventory - special arrangements, disposal/EPA standards, JIT capabilities

Research and Development: Capabilities, focus, i.e., customer, market, product, number of test runs to ensure consistency, R&D technical support

Customer Support Services: Order center, on-call 24 hours a day, customer service follow-up calls, marketing research for customer support, training, knowledgeable staff, technical support services, quick resolution of problems, documentation, warranties, guarantees, simplified paperwork, easy ordering process, customer interaction analysis

Sales: Customers to representative ratio, customer relationships, team approach, knowledge of customer's business, corporate account manager, "Partnering" relationships, national account manager, diagnostic and value-based approach to selling, accessibility, specialists, technical competence, responsive to customer needs

Your Case Study: Developing Your Competitor Analysis

Recall that the layout for the Competitor Analysis is best displayed in a box divided into four quadrants. You can use a sheet of paper to draw the boxes. It will make learning this process easier and more accurate.

While learning how to use the competitor analysis and how your results will work in the VSS P.R.O.S.P.E.C.T. Model, focus on the top three to five items in each quadrant.

- The **upper left quadrant** would contain the Customer Perceived Competitor's Strengths.
- The **upper right quadrant** would contain how your company neutralizes or offsets each competitor's advantages.
- The **lower left quadrant** would contain the competitor's weaknesses.
- The **lower right quadrant** would contain your company's strengths. Again, this is done on a one-to-one basis where you identify a strength for each of their weaknesses. These become your **Unique Selling Points (USPs)** when up against this competitor in this sales opportunity.

Unique Selling Points

Look at your areas of strength where your competitor has corresponding weaknesses. These areas of strength now become Unique Selling Points. They are:

- What your product, service, company, and you do that your competition does not do.

- They solve or prevent problems and have their Features, Advantages, and Benefits.
- They answer the question, "What makes you different from all the rest?"

To make your Unique Selling Points functional in the Value Selling Strategies process, they must be converted into Features, Advantages, and Benefits.

Features, Advantages & Benefits

Features are characteristics of your product, service, company, and self that serve a function to solve or prevent a problem.

Ask, "What is it?" The answer will give you the feature. For example, if you sold containers and asked, "What is it?" The answer, "It's a plastic container," would be a Feature.

Advantages tell why your features are a better way of providing benefits than the competitor. That is, they relate directly back to the feature. They help solve or prevent additional problems. They add value and help distinguish you from your competitors.

Ask, "Explain what that means?" The answer could be, "It's a plastic container so that it won't rust." This explanation tells you the function it serves and the Advantage of the feature over metal containers.

Benefits fill needs and motivate purchases. They tell what the customer will get that fills their business and, ultimately, human needs. Benefits are always directed to the customers.

Ask, "How will that lower your maintenance and replacement costs?

Needs that Motivate Purchase

Filling needs motivates purchase. There are **three categories of needs** to explore for the best fit:

Functional Needs
Business Needs
Human Needs

Your company buys products and services that fill functional needs to meet business needs, which are ultimately driven by the desire to fulfill fundamental human needs. The more needs you can meet in all three categories, the stronger your competitive position becomes.

Functional Needs

People buy things because they will fill some functional need that will, in turn, fill a business or human need. For example, a car jack will raise the car to change a flat tire, meeting the human need for safety. A remote control meets the functional need to change the channel without getting up, which meets human pleasure needs. An insulated cup meets the functional need to keep your beverages hot or cold, which then meets the pleasure need.

Companies fill their business needs by buying things that meet functional needs that, in turn, meet one or more of their four universal business needs. For example, purchasing self-cleaning equipment meets the efficiency need, or adding a new product to sell meets the profit need. All Advantages (Features, Advantages, and Benefits) meet a functional need, and all Benefits meet one or more business and human needs. Sometimes, the needs being filled are apparent; sometimes, they are not. You can always make them evident by how you write them.

For example, a plastic container won't rust (functional need), lowering the company's risk (security needs to minimize the risk) when they transfer the caustic material from the rusting container to a new one. Meeting the functional need (won't rust) also meets the efficiency need to reduce costs (do away with the replacement budget), and it meets the human needs of security and pleasure (not having to clean rust stains, transfer product, put on cumbersome safety gear, and so on).

Four Universal Business Needs

All businesses have four basic business needs.

1. Profit Needs: Increase the ability to generate profitable revenues.
2. Efficiency Needs: Reduce the costs of operation.
3. Security Needs: Lessen vulnerability in their marketplace and minimize internal risk.
4. Image Needs: Match company image to corporate and target market expectations.

Four Fundamental Human Needs

While each of the human needs can stand-alone as a motivator, they most often work in combination with other human needs to create another need. Human needs are the ultimate motivators.

1. Money Needs: Able to buy the necessities of life, such as food and shelter. Money can also be used to purchase symbols of success when coupled with esteem and pleasure needs.
2. Safety Needs: Freedom from fear of loss or harm to self, possessions, and others (persons or groups) with whom we identify. They can also include the needs for health, well-being, and power.
3. Esteem Needs: Feel confident in our ability to meet the challenges and solve the problems the world throws in front of us. Successful problem-solving abilities build and strengthen self-esteem. These also include our needs for love, affection, acceptance, confidence, and achievement.
4. Pleasure Needs: Living our passion, doing what we value, doing what we like to do. These activities (and purchases to support them) give us pleasure. Order, symmetry, closure, happiness, and beauty are also a part of these needs.

Human needs will influence a person's buying behavior, even when a business or functional need is the focus. This means you can let the prospect know you are helping them meet these human needs through your language when discussing your product or service. For example, if the business security needs are driving a purchase, you could use words such as warranty, solid, reliable, durable, and others to reinforce that you will meet this need. You could also point out how you minimize any personal risk (human safety needs) the buyer might incur because of sticking their necks out to buy from you.

You choose which needs to use (emphasize) based on what you discover about the company and the decision-makers with whom you interact.

Create the Criteria with FABs That Are USPs

The next step is converting the strengths (USPs) you identified in the competitor analysis into Features, Advantages, and Benefits (FABs). This persuasive language of selling will help you communicate through questions.

Case Study: The Jill Ryan Scenario

To illustrate this, let's return to Jill Ryan's Competitor Analysis and pull those areas where her company is strong and her competitor is weak.

Her areas of strength include:

- 24-hour, 7-day service availability
- Use telephone pre-call diagnostic questions
- Factory Certified technicians

Based on what you just learned, would you say these are Features, Advantages, or Benefits? They look like Features to me. So this means we must now define why her Features are a better way (Advantages) of delivering the Benefits.

Feature, Advantages, Benefits – Quick Review

Feature (F): characteristics of your product, service, company, or yourself.
Advantage (A): explains their function and tell why they're a better way to deliver Benefits.
Benefit (B): what the customer gets that fills their business and human needs

Jill's FABs

- **Feature (F)** - 24 / 7 service availability
- **Advantage (A)** - available when you need us
- **Benefit (B)** - decreases costly downtime waiting for service

- **F.** Telephone diagnostic process
- **A.** determine potential problems before leaving the shop so that they can select the right parts
- **B.** decrease trips to get parts and lessen costly downtime

- **F.** Factory-certified technicians
- **A.** know the equipment so they can get right to the problem
- **B.** reduce on-site service time and get you back into production, making money quicker

Reduce Benefits to Dollars

In Value Selling, priority should be given to reducing benefit statements to those that can be readily quantified in dollars. Particular attention is given to this process when working with the business needs. If you can't reduce it to dollars, then if there is a cutback, you may be the "line-item cost" that will have to go.

Complete Your FABs

Now, take some time to consider your USPs. Convert them into Features, Advantages, and Benefits as you see fit. A helpful strategy is to remove one of your company or product/service brochures and identify the Unique Selling Points' Features, Advantages, and Benefits.

Once you've done this, you can use your company's literature to guide your interview. If this is not available or incomplete, you'll want to develop your master list that you can select from and jot down on your "yellow pad" to guide your interview questions.

Sales Strategy

The intent of the Research Questions is to gain customer and competitor information to develop a win/win sales strategy.

We now have the necessary information.

1. We know our prospects' special needs by gaining information about the products/services they sell to generate revenues. We also know where and how we can impact the critical processes they use to have products/services to sell. We understand their needs from a big-picture perspective.
2. We know their business plan as it relates to what we sell. We see the timing from both the Profile question (buying cycle) and a research perspective. For example, based on what is important to us, this could include inventory on hand, usage rate, and knowing if they are going through an organizational change. We also know if the need for our products/services is increasing or decreasing.
3. We know about their selling environment. We know what they are up against in their marketplace. This enables us to know how to competitively advantage the customer in their marketplace.
4. Through the competitor analysis, we know which objections to expect

(from competitor's advantages) so that we can implement a strategy to "prevent" them from occurring and to respond to them as needed. We also know how to neutralize their strengths.

Additionally, we know where their weaknesses are and where we have strengths. Our primary strategy will be to focus our conversations with the prospect in those areas where we are strong, our competitor is weak, and the customer has needs.

Examples of Research Questions

Research the prospect's products and services.

- *Where or how in your product/service do you use what we sell?*
- *How does that impact what you sell?*
- *How can we make what we sell easier for you to sell?*
- *How would your customers respond to having _____ (USP)?*

Research the prospect's critical processes.

- *Could you briefly walk me through the process you use for your production line?*
- *How do you currently ________?*
- *Where are the bottlenecks that cause slow production?*
- *How would that impact the flow if you could apply _____ (USP)?*

Research the prospect's business plan.

- *Is your company proactive in this area?*
- *Is this a regularly budgeted product and service?*
- *Will you be expanding in this area?*
- *How frequently do you purchase this product/service?*
- *Do you use long-term supplier agreements?*

- *How do you handle the need to increase _______ (USP)?*

Identify your competitors.

- Are you using multiple suppliers for this product/service?
- *Who do you use as the supplier for this portion of the process?*
- Who are you currently using?
- Which of their products/services are you using?

Summary

Understanding your prospective customers from the perspective of the key decision-makers provides you with a wealth of information. Understanding your competitor's capabilities and limitations in this sales opportunity provides your sales strategy. From these two sets of information (customer & competitor), the rest of the sales process will unfold.

Keep in mind that you won't necessarily get all the information you want upfront. You will most likely pick up additional Profile and Research information throughout the sales process. That's why the P.R.O.S.P.E.C.T. Model is designed with great flexibility.

4

Orientation Questions

Intent

The intent of the Orientation Questions category is to focus on the topic of conversation in areas where you are strong, your competitor is weak, and the customer has needs.

Objectives

- Focus the conversation on exploring the prospect's priority areas of need where you are strong and your competitor is weak.
- Activate the strategy developed from information gained during the research phase.
- Zero in on specific areas that will lead to discovering direct or collateral problems you can solve with your Unique Selling Points.

Overview

During your Research Questions, you gained an understanding of how the products and services are currently used, the processes and steps involved in using them, and any potential areas where you might be able to improve their ability to meet one or more of the four business needs.

You also gained an understanding of their business plan timing and budgeting issues, as well as current and future goals as they relate to your products and services. And, you've gained an understanding of competing ways of doing what you sell. With the competitor analyses completed as necessary, you're now prepared to proceed with your interviews with the key decision-makers.

The Orientation Questions will activate the sales strategy developed in the Research Module. The objective is to orient the prospect to topics of conversation in areas where you are most likely to discover symptoms that will help diagnose problems you can solve with your unique selling points (USPs).

The priority areas to explore are those that are readily quantifiable and will directly result in lowering the prospect's cost of operation and increasing their ability to generate revenues. You orient the prospect in areas where you are strong, the competitor is weak, and the customer has needs.

How to Build Orientation Questions

The Orientation Question is formulated by looking at the Feature of the first unique selling point you translated into the Feature, Advantage, and Benefit format.

Ask, *"How could I introduce this as a general topic of discussion?"*

Case Study: The Jill Ryan Scenario

Jill will need to activate her sales strategy by getting the prospect to focus on areas where her company is strong, the competitor is weak, and the customer has needs. Remember, this information was obtained during the Research Questions.

The first step will be to define the features of her USPs in functional terms or as a topic. For Example:

Orientation Topic: ***Hours of operation***

F. 24-hour service, 7 days a week

A. available after regular work hours and on weekends

B. less downtime

Orientation Topic: ***Service call planning***

F. telephone troubleshooting process

A. bring the right parts to the site

B. decrease downtime waiting on parts

Orientation Topic: ***Technician qualifications***

F. certified technicians

A. know the equipment, can get right to the problem

B. reduce on-site service time

How to Ask Orientation Questions

"Jill Ryan" Case Study Examples:

1. Simply ask the prospect to discuss a specific area.
I'd like to focus for a moment in the area of repair service hours of operation.

2. After a discussion with another person, you would use this type of question or statement to orient the prospect.
I talked to Mr. Jones yesterday, and he indicated that your hours of operation had been increased and that you've added a third shift.

3. Provide the prospect with choices from which to select. You do this by simply listing three of your topic/function areas.
Based on what you've told me, I have three areas I'd like to address:

   1. *The first area would be your requirements for the qualifications of the technicians you allow to work on your equipment.*

2. *The second relates to the hours of operation in which you need services.*
3. *And the third area relates to the service call planning done before the technician travels to the site.*

Which of these would you like to discuss first?

4. Ask the prospect to explore a "narrowly defined" process, which you know from competitive experience will be filled with clues (symptoms).

Could you tell me more about the specific process you use to get repair services on all three shifts?

5. Introduce the topic of discussion and connect it to a Symptom Question.

When thinking about your hours of operation, what are your greatest concerns about repair service availability after regular work hours and on weekends?

Fill in the Blanks Practice

Simply ask the prospect to discuss a specific area.

I'd like to focus for a moment in the area of ________.

After a discussion with another person, you would use this type of question to orient the prospect.

I talked to Mr. Jones yesterday, and he indicated that ________.

Provide the prospect with choices from which to select. You do this by simply listing three of your topic/function areas.

Based on what you've told me, I have three areas I'd like to address:

1. ______________________________,
2. ______________________________,
3. ______________________________.

Which of these would you like to discuss first?

Ask the prospect to explore a narrowly defined process, which you know from competitive experience will be filled with clues (symptoms).

Could you tell me more about the specific process you use to ________?

Introduce the topic of discussion and connect it to a Symptom Question.

In thinking about your _____, what are your greatest concerns related to _____?

Your Case Study

Now it's time to look at three of your Unique Selling Points (USP) that you expanded into the persuasive language of selling, which we call Features, Advantages, and Benefits.

Look at the Feature and go up a level or to more of a generalized representation, and think about the category or topic that specific feature might fall under. This would be like telling the customer that you want to talk about your capability and the competitor's capability in an area. What would you call that area without using the name of either your Feature or the competitor's Feature? This is the general topic of discussion you would orient the conversation with the prospective customer.

For example, *"Based on what we've talked about, three areas raise a red flag for me, 1. ______, 2. _______ and 3. _______* (USPs). *Which would you like to talk about first?"*

Summary

Look at the lower right quadrant of your competitor analysis. Those are the areas where you initially want to orient the prospective customer. Look at each item and ask yourself how you could introduce it as a general topic of discussion rather than a specific Feature.

The next step is to bring up the topic as one you'd like to focus your discussion on for a moment. It's just that simple.

5

Symptom Questions

Intent

The intent of the Symptom Questions category is to identify both the obvious and the hidden needs not currently being met by the competitor.

Objectives

- Identify obvious needs.
- Uncover the hidden needs not being met by the competitor.
- Work with the prospect to discover potential needs for new or modified products/services.
- Begin to move the prospect out of their comfort zone.
- Prevent the prospect from denying a problem exists.
- Preempt or answer the prospect's/customer's question, "What makes you think I've got a problem?

Overview

The Symptom Questions help you, directly and indirectly, uncover problems the prospect may have that your product or service can solve. If you don't find a problem, the prospect will not need your product or service. Symptoms support the contention that a problem does indeed exist.

Quite often, if you ask the prospect directly if a problem exists or if they have a need, they will say NO! Why? For three fundamental reasons:

- They may have a way of dealing with it (cumbersome and costly, perhaps).
- They may not want to admit to a problem.
- They may not know they have a problem.

The Symptom Questions ensure we can prevent or answer the customer's question, "What makes you think I have a problem?"

Psychologically speaking, busy people have enough problems, and unless this particular problem is screaming for attention, the tendency is not to look for trouble. Just as when you have pain such as a slight toothache, you may discover that the pain disappears during the day when you are dealing with major problems at work that require your full attention.

This happens because you are distracted from one pain (the toothache) when focused on a bigger pain (a significant challenge at work). When the bigger pain is dealt with, the toothache pain returns and will continue to do so until it gets bad enough to reach the top of the priority list.

Therefore, by simply calling attention to the symptoms, you bring the pain to conscious awareness. Only here can the prospect feel it. This will get the prospect's full attention. The more symptoms you uncover, the higher the priority becomes to do something about it.

Where to Find Symptoms

In looking for symptoms, we return to our features, advantages, and benefits. Recall that a feature serves a function that solves a problem. If the prospect does not use your product/service, they do not have your Unique Selling Point's Feature. They will not receive the related Advantages and Benefits if they do not have the Feature.

What you look for are the missing Advantages and Benefits of your Unique Selling Points. These are the visible symptoms.

The process then, for developing Symptom Questions, is to first look at the problems your product and service solve. Then, ask, "What symptoms suggest the prospect has this problem?" Or, "What would I see if the prospect doesn't have the Advantages and Benefits delivered by my Unique Selling Points Feature?"

Case Study: The Jill Ryan Scenario

What might you see if the prospect does not have 24-hour service available seven days a week and the prospect's operation is 24 hours, seven days a week when breakdowns occur after regular business hours? Remember from the Profile and Research Questions the prospect is using J.I.T. delivery, and neither the prospect nor the customers have storage space.

Clues

Look for the clues, signs, or symptoms that will help answer the prospect's question, "What makes you think I've got a problem?"

Look for the clues, signs, or symptoms that will help answer the prospect's question, "What makes you think I've got a problem?"

Jill's FAB

F. 24-hour service, 7 days a week

A. available after regular work hours and on weekends

B. less downtime

Symptoms: Missing Advantages & Benefits

- Don't meet production goals due to downtime in excess of the actual repair time.
- Downtime due to waiting for repair service.

Orientation: *"I'd like to focus for a moment in the area of repair service hours of operation:*

Symptom: *"...when your equipment goes down after regular work hours or on the weekend, what are your greatest concerns related to*

- *Downtime in excess of the usual repair time?*
- *Missing production goals?"*

Jill's FAB

F. pre-call telephone troubleshooting process

A. bring the right parts to the site

B. decrease downtime waiting on parts

Symptoms: Missing Advantages & Benefits

- Service people must return to their shops to get the right parts.
- Downtime waiting

Orientation: *"I talked to Mr. Jones yesterday, and he indicated that the repair technicians didn't get any specific information about the equipment before they came out to the worksite*

Symptom: *"...what are the headaches created when they don't have the right parts to make the repair?"*

Jill's FAB

F. certified technicians

A. knows the equipment, can get right to the problem

B. reduce on-site service time

Symptoms: Missing Advantages & Benefits

- Hit or miss repairs.
- Sometimes, they break parts trying to figure out how it works.
- Takes more time to find and fix the problems.

Orientation: *"In thinking about the qualifications of the technicians you have working on your equipment*

Symptom: *"...what are your greatest areas of concern, particularly when it comes to the amount of time it takes and getting the repair right the first time?"*

How to Ask Symptom Questions

Remember, you are looking for clues that suggest a problem exists. In doing this, be very careful not to use the word "problem." Using the word "problem" at this stage of the interview may cause the prospect to become defensive, deny their existence, or simply not know of any.

The plan is not to use the word "problem" until after you've substantiated the existence of a problem with the symptoms.

With the Orientation Questions, the prospect agreed to focus their attention in areas where your competitor is weak and you are strong. This will ensure that we find symptoms.

General Symptom Question Examples

You might want to simply Orient the prospect to an area and then ask Symptom Questions such as, *"In thinking about ______, what are your greatest areas of concern?"*

Remember that the Orientation Question focuses the topic of conversation in an identified area so that the following general questions are not just loose but directly associated with a specific topic.

"What about this gives you the biggest headaches?"

"What takes up most of your time?"

"Where's the pain?"

"What are your greatest concerns related to _____?"

"Tell me about that."

"What's going on in that area?"

"What do you see here?"

Symptom questions are phrased positively. Orient then:

"What would make it better for you?"

"How much additional profit could be added when this is done?"

"In thinking about the speed of the equipment and the backlog you're facing, how would increasing the output by 50% improve the profit margin?"

Where's the pain, or where's the gain? They both work well.

And, you can imply the current supplier is not up to par with what you can provide.

For example, *"In thinking about the speed of the equipment and the backlog you're facing, what are your greatest concerns about being unable to improve productivity over what you have now?"*

Your Case Study

Look at the advantages and benefits you listed, then determine what you might see if the prospect does not have these Advantages and Benefits. Ask yourself, "What makes me think they have a problem that requires my USP's Feature to solve?"

TIP: Write just one or two words or, at most, a brief phrase. Then, use the "fill in the blank" examples.

Summary

The Symptom Questions substantiate that a problem exists that is not being solved by the competitor. Now, there may come a time when you have a strength to a competitor's weakness, and when you ask, you don't uncover any symptoms, then you might suspect that the customer truly has a need there and has found some way to compensate for it. Your job now is to identify how they're compensating and at what cost.

6

Problem Questions

Intent

The intent of the Problem Question category is to define the root causes of the symptoms and confirm the existence of problems.

Objectives

- Identify and get agreement on the root cause of the symptoms.
- Confirm the existence of problems.
- Define the problem as one you can solve with a unique selling point.
- Define the problem, or potential problem, as one that may lead to developing a modified or new product or service.

Overview

Before a person buys a solution, they must first agree and acknowledge that they have a problem or at least have some reasonable potential for a problem. For example, why do people buy accident insurance? They purchase insurance because there is some reasonable probability that an accident could occur.

The problem does not have to be real. It must simply have some reasonable probability of occurring within a given time frame.

The two primary purposes of this question are to:

- Point the symptoms toward the problems you can solve with your products and services USPs.
- Get the prospect to admit to having a problem.

Recall the problem does not have to be real; it only needs a reasonable probability of occurring.

Caution is given not to present solutions once the problem has been defined. To do so will invite the "price" objection and may cause the prospect to seek out one of your competitor's lower-cost solutions. Remember, there will always be someone cheaper.

Where to Diagnose Problems

The problem is always diagnosed or defined in terms that reflect the general category or function of your Feature. This is like the topic or functional area you used in your Orientation Question, but now it is stated as a deficit or "not having," for example.

The **problem is that the prospect does not have your USP's Feature**, and that's why they don't have your Advantages and Benefits, which show up as symptoms.

Suppose your conversation meanders as you explore a set of symptoms to diagnose a problem. In that case, it might be advisable to summarize the symptoms and then directly connect that summary to the problem diagnosis.

Developing Problem Questions

There are several ways to connect the missing Feature to the missing Advantages and Benefits, which show up as Symptoms. One key term is "not having" the Feature (generically stated). For example, "That pain could be a problem caused by not having my product's Unique Selling Point's Feature." Okay, you may have to replace some words, but you get the point.

Confirming the existence of the problem includes not only diagnosing it but also getting the prospect to confirm that diagnosis. To do this, you might use a simple Rhetorical Question Close, such as, "Isn't it?" "Doesn't it?" "Couldn't it?" "Don't you agree?" "That makes sense, doesn't it?" and so on. You could also use the non-verbal Rhetorical close. This is simply making a statement, then moving your head up and down to signify "Yes." This works when rapport is well established. To stay in rapport, the person would necessarily need to mirror and match your behavior or suffer the psychological discomfort that occurs when rapport is lost.

Summarize Symptoms and Diagnose the Problem

- *"If your repairs seem to be hit or miss and the technicians are taking more time and causing more damage trying to fix it right, then that points to a problem with not using certified technicians to do the work, doesn't it?"*

Sometimes, it is not necessary to summarize the symptoms. You could just diagnose.

- *"That could be a problem with not using trained and certified technicians, couldn't it?"*
- *"That sounds like a problem worth exploring further, doesn't it?"*

If you are exploring new products/services, then you might ask:

- *"How would you define what we see here?"*

- *"What do you think is causing this?"*

Summarize one or two of the clear symptoms you have identified, then diagnose the problem using the general topic category or function of the feature as missing.

- *"So, if you're seeing this and not getting that, then that could be a problem with not having _____, right?"*

The Problem Question can also be used as a transition to the next category of questions to begin to explore how serious the problem is. (Effects/Consequences)

I'm not sure how significant this problem is, but at least it's worth looking into the effects it may be having.

- *"This might be a serious problem for you. Let's look at it a little more closely, okay?"*

Case Study: The Jill Ryan Scenario

To set up the following examples, let's detail the first one in which the prospect's current supplier only offers services from 7 AM to 6 PM. Here, clear symptoms were uncovered. Those symptoms included excessive downtime during a breakdown after regular working hours. The problem is that they are not using a repair service company that operates the same hours they do.

Jill's FAB

F. 24-hour, 7-day service

A. available when you need service

B. less downtime

Summarize Symptoms

"So, if you see production goals not met and excessive downtime waiting for the

regular work week to start, then that..."

Problem Diagnosis

"...points to a problem with not having service available around the clock seven days a week, doesn't it?"

Jill's FAB

F. phone troubleshooting process

A. bring the right parts to call

B. decrease downtime

Summarize Symptoms

"If the technician has to return to get the right parts and you're experiencing downtime while you're waiting, that..."

Problem Diagnosis

"...points to a problem with not using a troubleshooting process over the phone before coming on-site, simple as that." (Statement made with confidence and head moving up and down, signifying the "non-verbal" rhetorical question close).

Jill's FAB

F. certified technicians

A. know what to do

B. reduce service time

Summarize Symptoms

"If your repairs seem to be hit and miss and the technicians are taking more time and are causing more damage trying to fix it right, then that..."

Problem Diagnosis

"...points to a problem with not using certified technicians to do the work, doesn't it?"

Your Case Study

For a quick practice, summarize the symptoms and say, *"...that points to a problem with not having* ______ (state the function or topic of the Feature). Now confirm that with a Rhetorical Question Close, such as, "Doesn't it?" "Don't you agree?" "That makes sense, doesn't it?" and so on.

Summary

The Problem is the missing Feature that provides the Advantages and Benefits which are also missing. Those Benefits fill needs, and those unfilled needs, when brought to the person's attention, cause discomfort. The Feature, Advantage, and Benefit are all missing because the prospect isn't currently doing business with you and consequently doesn't have your Unique Selling Point. I'm hoping you're beginning to see how circular this is becoming and how vital the Competitor Analysis is in identifying your USPs). I'm also hoping you're starting to understand how important it is to convert your USPs into Features, Advantages, and Benefits.

7

Effects / Consequences Question

Intent

The intent of the Effects / Consequences Questions category is to quantify the seriousness of the problem to establish the value of the solution and determine the future costs associated with not solving the problem.

Objectives

- Eliminate duplicate and collateral costs for the customer by improving efficiency with your Unique Selling Points.
- Gain customer understanding regarding special price requests by quantifying the costs of the customer's current methods using the customer's facts and figures.
- Identify and quantify the hidden costs of using the competing company to offset and justify a premium price.
- Focus on actual bottom-line value, which includes the "cost to get" and the "cost to use."
- Prevent "price" and "stall" type objections.
- Create a sense of urgency and put the pressure of time on the customer by quantifying the consequences of not solving the problems with your

Unique Selling Points.
- Establish the basis to determine the customer's return on investment.

Overview

Your Unique Selling Points (USP) have features that serve functions that solve problems. The prospect has confirmed the existence of these problems. It would be tempting to tell the prospect how we can help solve them. And yet, at this time, we must still refrain from presenting our solutions. Why?

Think about all the problems every one of us has. Ask yourself, "Why not just solve them all right now?" The answers include:

- Don't have enough time and money
- Have to set priorities on what we can do now with the available resources
- Is the solution I'm looking at the best one?

Now that the prospect has admitted to a problem or the potential for a problem, the questions become:

- How serious is the problem?
- How valuable is the solution?

Effects/Consequences questions establish the value of the solution

Effects define and quantify the past and current impact the problem is having on the prospect's ability to achieve their objectives.

Consequences define and quantify losses incurred if the problem is not resolved.

Where to Find the Effects/Consequences

Our challenge is to discover what it costs the prospect not to have the Advantages and Benefits of our USP Features. A feature serves a function that solves a problem.

If the prospect is not using your product/service, they do not have your unique selling point's feature. They will not receive the related Advantages and Benefits if they do not have this Feature.

The prospect has admitted they have a problem that can only be solved with your USPs. Your next step is quantifying the impact of the missing Advantages and Benefits. This will establish the value of the feature.

Developing Effects / Consequences Questions

Unless we know the value of what we sell, it won't be easy to sell value to the customer.

In determining value, it is vital to calculate the cost to use your product/service relative to the cost to use your competitor's product/service or the cost to use neither.

There are four basic ways to determine value:

1. What is the perceived value of your unique selling point? If you perceive it as valuable, then your belief and enthusiasm will transfer to the prospect - just as a perception on your part that it is not valuable will also transfer. This is known as the "self-fulfilling prophecy."
2. What is the Return on Investment (ROI)? How does your unique selling point impact the customer's cost to "get and use" the bottom line? What does it cost the customer, out of their current budget, not to have the advantages and benefits of your unique selling point? See ROI Below.
3. What is the collective value of the package you sell? Your ability to unbundle and repackage, specifically to the customer's needs, has value to you and the customer.

4. What is the subjective value the customer gives to your Unique Selling Points?

Cost/Benefit Analysis - Return on Investment (R.O.I.)

In selling, the cost/benefit analysis is used to answer the question, *"Did the value of the advantages and benefits offset the cost of the feature that provides them?"* If, for example, one of the benefits is time-saving, then the question becomes, *"How much time will need to be saved, over what period, and at what rate, before the feature pays for itself and begins to provide us with a return on our investment?"*

- Specifiers need help to cost-justify their expenditures.
- Final Authorities need to see the cost/value ratio to determine if this is the place to put the company's money or if some other investment would bring a better return on that investment (ROI), a better rate of return (ROR), or a better return on assets (ROA).
- Negotiators look primarily at top-line prices and, for the most part, are not interested in the overall value to the company. Sometimes, in purchasing departments where they may buy 10,000-line items, they don't know what they're buying does for the company. So, they use certain rules of thumb, such as the more Features a product or service has, the more they are willing to spend on it. The more the salesperson can educate them about their product and service, the more trust they will place in it, and the more likely they will select it.

Subjective Value

Many benefits people receive are sometimes subjective and do not readily render themselves to a "dollar" amount. Subjective feelings such as peace of mind, increased feelings of security, increased comfort, higher esteem, and so on versus frustrations, feelings of uncertainty, or greater risk all have a tremendous impact on buying decisions. Therefore, they must be identified and included.

In the Criteria/Benefits Questions module, you will see how the Benefits Questions are designed to help you obtain this "personal value" information.

Any value-selling process must prevent price objections with objective facts and figures. Therefore, focus on quantifiable data during this part of the interview. Note that some subjective information can be translated into measurable data. For example, if a product is unreliable, the customer may stock additional inventory above and beyond what would be normally expected. The cost of the money tied up in this inventory can now be calculated.

Intangible Real Value - Current Methods - Your Company

- Feelings of security
- Frustration and anxiety
- Comfort level
- Ease of operation
- Risk factors

Examples of Effects/Consequences Questions

Whenever you ask a quantification-type question, you are asking an Effects Question. Whenever that question speaks to the future costs associated with not solving the problem, you are asking a Consequence Question. Be sure to identify and list the items you will quantify.

Financial Value

- *"How does that affect your ability to meet your production goals?"*
- *"How often does it happen?"*
- *"How much time does it take?"*
- *"How many people are involved?"*
- *"What is the hourly rate of pay?"*
- *"What is the salary burden?" (Note that the benefits package is minimally 20% and can sometimes double the pay rate.)*

- *"How much of the risk factor would be reduced if the problem were addressed?"*
- *"These problems could be expensive to fix; let's do a cost/benefit analysis to see if there is sufficient justification to move ahead. Let's begin with..."*
- *"What does that mean over the next 12 months?"*
- *"Is that something you've identified in your budget for next year?"*
- *"If we look at these costs and savings over the contract's life, it looks as though your R.O.I. will be close to a 10:1 ratio. That will get the support to move ahead, won't it?"*

Subjective Value

- *"How does that impact their feelings of security?"*
- *"How frustrating is that?"*
- *"What happens to your comfort level?"*
- *"How easy is this to operate?"*
- *"What risk factors are you faced with using this procedure?"*

Case Study: The Jill Ryan Scenario

Whenever you ask a quantification-type question, you are asking an Effects Question. Whenever that question speaks to the future costs associated with not solving the problem, you are asking a Consequence Question.

The prospect-related during the Research Questions that they are averaging about ten service calls per month equally averaged among the three shifts.

The current suppliers charge $80 per hour, while Ryan's company charges $125 per hour. To level the financial playing field, Jill must now help the prospect discover what it costs not to have the advantages and benefits of her Unique Selling Points.

Effects/Consequences Questions - Criteria for Selection

Jill's FAB

F. 24-hour, 7-day service

A. available when you need service

B. less downtime

Effects/Consequences Questions

- *"How often do you have breakdowns after regular business hours or on weekends?"*
- *"What is the average amount of time you are down monthly?"*
- *"How much of that downtime was spent waiting for the repair service to open for business?"*
- *"What does an hour of production cost?"*

Jill's FAB

F. telephone troubleshooting process

A. bring the right parts to call

B. decrease downtime

Effects/Consequences Questions

- *"On average, how often do the repair service people have to return to their shops to get the right parts?"*
- *"How long does it take them to drive back to the shop, get the parts, and return?"*

Jill's FAB

F certified technicians

A know what to do

B reduces service time

Effects/Consequences Questions

- *"How long does it usually take for repairs to be made?"*
- *"How many times have additional parts been damaged during the repair*

operation?"

- *"What are the costs associated with these additional items?"*

Balance Sheet

Suppose you were to add the additional costs associated with not having Jill's USPs and add them to the cost of the competitor's offering. In that case, you'd very clearly see (as would the prospect) that $80 per hour is at the bottom-line level, more expensive than the $125 per hour rate that Jill's company charges.

Standards of Legitimacy

Use this when the prospect doesn't know the numbers. Standards of legitimacy are your norms or industry standards.

In many sales situations, you will find yourself interviewing people who really are unaware of the actual costs associated with doing specific tasks. As such, you must be prepared with the "standards of legitimacy" for these costs or risk having the sale stall while the prospect looks up the numbers.

A standard of legitimacy is a rule of thumb or guideline used to establish the cost of certain key areas your product or service impacts. For example, if your product/service saves time, it is important to know whose time it saves, how much time it saves, and how much that time is worth.

If, for example, your product/service saves 4 hours per week of a technician's time and the prospect does not know how much technicians earn per hour, then you will need to provide a temporary guideline. You can determine this from industry magazines, newspapers, "Help Wanted ads," personnel staff, and so on, as well as what the "average" technician (manager, clerk, etc.) earns on an hourly basis plus benefits.

In this example, let's say that a technician earns $15.00 per hour, and the benefits package and overhead run about 50% of the pay rate. Therefore, 1.5 X $15.00 = $22.50 per hour.

Time savings with your product or service of 4 hours per week for 52 weeks would be 208 person-hours. Multiply the 208 person-hours by the hourly rate of $22.50 you get $4,680.00. This amount becomes a "hidden" cost to be added to the cost of using your competitor's product/service.

Therefore, if the item you sell is priced at $12,000 and your competitor charges $10,000, we must now add to the competitor's price the hidden use costs of $4,680 to obtain the same results you get. So now, the actual bottom line for your competitor's product or service is $14,680 versus your $12,000.

Item / Current Methods / Your Company

Price to get the Product/Service: Current methods: $10,000 versus your company: $12,000

Cost to USE (extra man-hours): Current methods: + $4,680 versus your company: + $0

Bottom Line Value: Current methods: $14,680 versus your company: $12,000

With this information displayed in a side-by-side comparison format, what happens to the often-heard objection? *"Your price is much higher than your competitor's?"* or, *"I can get it cheaper elsewhere."*

Setting the Standards of Legitimacy with the Prospect

The process is simply offering a number based on your norms or industry standards and then negotiating a reasonable figure to use during the calculations.

You might say, "Most technicians with four years' experience earn in the neighborhood of $15 per hour plus about a 50% benefits and overhead package, bringing that to $22.50 per hour. Is that about right for the technicians we're talking about, or are they a little higher or lower?"

You can continue the process once the prospect accepts the figure you and they agree upon. Remember, the prospect can verify the figures later, but the sale moves forward for now.

Consequences

In this example, the consequences for not changing to your product or service are a financial loss of $390 per month out of the current budget and, over the next five years, will cost the prospect an additional $23,400 to continue to use your competitor's product or service.

Item: Current Methods versus Your Company

Additional Cost to Use: $4,680 versus $0

Multiplied by volume or product life over the length of the agreement (X 5 years) = $______.

Total additional USE costs: $23,400 versus $0

\+ **Price to Get:** $10,000 versus $12,000

= **Bottom Line Budget Impact:** $33,400 versus $12,000

Important Note: During the P.R.O.S.P.E.C.T. interview, you will only be gathering information for the current methods. You will introduce the "get" and "use" cost comparison for your products/services during the Customer Value Proposition.

Your Case Study

So, look at the Advantages and Benefits of the first FAB you wrote and ask yourself, "What does (will) it cost the prospect if they don't have this?"

Next, ask, "What am I basing that on? Is it productivity, hourly wage, salary burden, or what?" Here, you are attempting to identify the "standards of legitimacy" you're using to build your business case for purchasing from you.

During negotiations, very often, what is actually being negotiated are the standards selected to determine value.

Using these standards and the anticipated life of the product, how much additional will the prospect pay for not having the Advantages and Benefits of your Unique Selling Point's (USP) Feature?

Note, you can use the product's life, warranty period, savings, or increased profits each month and calculate these until you quickly close the gap between your higher cost to get (price) and theirs.

Caution that you don't quantify more than three times the difference. Why? Because if you do, the numbers can quickly become "unbelievable," weakening trust and the accompanying feelings of security. The sale becomes less viable once fear, uncertainty, and doubt (FUD) enter the equation.

Summary

The Effects/Consequences Questions help you quantify your solution's financial and subjective value to each specific customer. Effects measure the past and current value, and the Consequences measure the future costs if the problem is not solved.

You quantify what it costs not to have the Advantages and Benefits of your Unique Selling Points that can solve a painful and now recognized costly problem.

It should be clear that your solution's value could vary from customer to customer based on how many of your USPs are critical for them and based on the Standards of Legitimacy agreed upon. For example, if in one company, the burdened hourly rate is $25 and, in another company, it's $15, it won't take too many hours to see a significant difference.

8

Criteria/Benefit Question

Intent

The intent of the Criteria/Benefits Questions category is to get agreement on the requirements that must be met to select a solution and to get the customer to rehearse a defense of the criteria.

Objectives - Criteria Questions

- Define, set, and agree on the requirements that must be met to solve the identified problems.
- Include your Unique Selling Points in the criteria to rule out the competition.
- Focus attention on solutions.
- Lay the foundation for the "Competitive Comparison Close."

Objectives - Benefit Questions

- Discover true buying motives important to the customer.
- Rehearse the prospect to sell internally for you when you are not around.
- Rehearse the customer to defend the criteria and turn changeable beliefs

into resistant attitudes.

- Enable the customer to make the claims for receiving benefits rather than you making them.
- Prevent skepticism-type objections.
- Identify others in the customer's organization who will also receive benefits.

Important Note: Although we will learn about the Criteria Questions and the Benefit Questions separately in this module, these two questions are tied together. As you will learn, a Benefit Question should not be asked unless directly tied to criteria (singular or multiple).

Overview

At this point, we have defined a problem and established what it costs the prospect not to have the advantages and benefits of your USPs features that would solve the problem. However, we must continue to refrain from presenting at this time because we have not yet established the criteria for selecting a solution.

Once the prospect sets and defends the criteria (Benefits Questions), you can present how to meet them.

Criteria Questions: Set the criteria to solve the problems that you and your competitors must meet. These criteria will include your USPs. Criteria Questions help the prospect rule out the competition.

Benefit Questions: Discover primary buying motives, rehearse the prospect to defend the criteria, and sell internally for you when you are not around. Benefit Questions help the prospect to lock out the competition.

The Criteria/Benefits Questions establish the selection criteria for buying your type of product and service. The criteria must include your Unique Selling Points. By including your Unique Selling Points and getting the prospect to state that they wouldn't consider a product/service without them effectively allows the prospect to rule out the competition.

TO WIN A SALE, THE RESEARCH SHOWS YOU ONLY NEED 5 +/- 2 USPs fully quantified and set as Criteria.

Options for the word Criteria

Although some have slightly different meanings and have various levels of strength, the following words are interchangeable with "criteria," including requirements, specifications, expectations, standards, objectives, or conditions.

Criteria include the requirements defined by the "Total Quality Management" process. They also encompass other areas that make doing business with your company preferred over doing business with your competitors, who might also meet the customer's requirements.

Recognize that while an "objective" may not be a "requirement" in the strictest sense of the word, it can become one of the "criteria" for supplier selection. While each of these terms has a different slant in meaning, they can all become part of the criteria.

The objective of the Criteria Question is to help you set your USPs as a part of the overall selection criteria. Once accepted by the customer, then both you and the competitor must be able to meet them. Since they are your USPs, you can certainly meet them; however, your competitors will not. Consequently, the customer will rule out your competitor from this sale.

Criteria Questions

State the criteria in terms of the features, advantages, and benefits of your product/service capable of solving each of the problems uncovered so that it becomes clear that when these criteria are met, the quantified effects/consequences will be reduced or eliminated. Give priority to setting those criteria that are readily quantifiable.

Developing Criteria Questions

- Use the function or category of the feature as the criteria.
- Further, explain the feature by stating its advantages and benefits. This supports how the effects and consequences will be reduced or eliminated.
- Confirm and get agreement on the criteria.

For example, *"So one of your criteria when selecting a supplier would be that they could provide you with [FAB]. Is that pretty much how you see it?"*

Notice that you state the criteria in general terms, explain it with the Advantage, and then provide the Benefit to solve the problem and reduce the Effects and Consequences. Once done, you then use some form of Rhetorical Question closing strategy ("Isn't it?" Wasn't it? Couldn't it? Shouldn't it? Is that how you see it? Right?).

Using our earlier barrel example sitting in the salt air:

F: Made of plastic

A: Won't rust

B: Fewer replacements

"Given the number of barrels you have to replace each year and your goal to lower your replacement budget, one of your criteria for selecting a supplier is that they would be able to provide you with barrels made of plastic so they won't rust away and that will, in turn, lower your replacement budget. Is that pretty much how you see it?"

Irrefutable Logic as Basic Proof of Capability

You utilize circular and irrefutable logic as basic proof. In setting your Feature's function as Criteria, you have come full circle in the formula.

1. You oriented the prospect to your USP's feature's function. The symptoms you and the prospect uncovered were what you would see when the

advantages and benefits of this feature are missing.

2. The problem is then quite naturally defined as the missing function of the feature. You then quantified what it costs the prospect not to have your advantages and benefits. This increased the priority of this problem. Doing this also prevented price objections and stalls.
3. At this time, it is clear to the prospect that the way to solve the problem (to clear up the symptoms and reduce or eliminate the associated costs) is to set the function of your USP's feature as one of the criteria to select a solution.

By double-checking your features, advantages, and benefits for clear internal logic, the logic expressed through the P.R.O.S.P.E.C.T. model will stand independently.

This doesn't mean having outside "proof" such as testimonials, references, test data, and other supporting documentation isn't important. These forms of proof should be only used to support the logical conclusion, not make it.

Advantages of "irrefutable logic"

- The P.R.O.S.P.E.C.T. model enables you to capitalize on using irrefutable logic. Its structure requires it to be used. The advantages of this process are many.
- How could you introduce a new or improved product or service without it? There would be no time to build a track record in all the different companies of different sizes and the market segments you sell to. With this process, the proof is in the logic. With the Benefits questions tied in, the prospect makes the claims, not you.
- New companies and new salespeople benefit because establishing the logic is question-driven. The salesperson does not need to be experienced. They only need solid company, product/service, and competitor knowledge.
- The prospect is the expert and usually feels that their company is "different" than anyone else you call on. Therefore, all your research studies to prove performance may be true for "others," but probably not here.

This system uses irrefutable logic to make a point or draw a conclusion. Research and testimonials only support the conclusion, not make it.

- If you make a claim, you must prove it.
- The speed at which the sales process can move is increased dramatically when the questions are combined and even pantomimed or otherwise acted out.

Example of irrefutable Logic FAB in Action

Let's use the plastic barrels once again to illustrate irrefutable or irreducible logic.

Feature: Made of plastic

Advantage: Won't rust

Benefit: No replacement costs due to rust

To test if the logic is irrefutable, say it backward, then start in the middle and see if it still makes sense. For example, you can stop spending money on replacing those barrels by buying some made of a material such as plastic that won't rust.

To continue with the illustration, the Research Questions showed that the prospective customer was spending a lot of money to replace rusty containers.

Conversational sales interview example.

Seller: [O] *"Let's focus for a moment on the materials your containers are made from."*

Buyer: *"Okay."*

Seller: [S] *"What are your greatest concerns related to them rusting?"*

Buyer: [P] *"That's a big problem for us. We have to replace a lot of them for that very reason."*

Seller: [E] *"How many do you replace each year, and at what cost?"*

Buyer: *"We average around 1,000 replacements at around $100 each."*

Seller: [E] *"Does that include the man-hours to make the change and the disposal costs of the rusted containers."*

Buyer: *"No, those costs would add another 30% or $130 each."*

Seller: [**E/C**] *"So you have somewhere in your budget a line-item cost of around $100,000 plus another $30,000 hidden in other budgets?"*

Buyer: *"Yeah, I guess so; I never thought about it that way."*

Seller: [**C/B**] *"So, one of your Criteria for selecting a supplier is that they could provide containers made of some material that won't rust, thereby saving that amount from your budget. Is that pretty much how you see it?"*

Buyer: *"Yes, I guess so."*

Seller: [**E/C**] *"And if we look at the useful life of the product in the container, you're estimating around five years, so that would be a total of $650,000 savings?"*

Buyer: *"At least that amount."*

Seller: [**C/B**] *"In addition to what we've discussed, what other benefits would you or your team get from not having to replace those barrels?"*

Buyer: *"First, replacing the barrels is a nasty job, and no one likes to do it. Second, if there is a spill, we have to call management, and then, over time, paperwork and frustration take over."*

Seller: [**T**] *"So I guess our next step is for me to present how we can meet your criteria and then look at how we can ensure we meet all the other specifications for the containers. Next, we'll..."*

Case Study: The Jill Ryan Scenario

To further illustrate how setting the criteria completes the "irrefutable logic" loop, let's return to Jill Ryan's meeting with Mr. Simms, Vice-President of Operations in the food processing plant.

F. 24 hour, 7-day service

A. available when you need service

B. less downtime

Ryan: *"Mr. Simms, based on what we've discovered here, one of your criteria that would have to be met would be having a supplier with a* ***24-hour service, seven days a week*** *so that they would be available for your after-hours and weekend calls to reduce the costs associated with downtime in excess of normal travel and on-site repair time, is that pretty much how you see it?"*

Simms: *"Absolutely, we just can't afford this anymore, and with the equipment getting older and requiring more service, this requirement will have to be met."*

F telephone troubleshooting process

A. bring the right parts to call

B decrease downtime

Ryan: *"Another important condition for your supplier is that they take the time to conduct some brief troubleshooting over the phone so they can arrive on the job with the right parts?"*

Simms: *"That goes without saying, but since we didn't say it before, and we're not getting it, we'll make sure that goes into the specifications package."*

F certified technicians

A know what to do

B reduces service time.

Ryan: *"Finally, the amount of service time and accidental breakage we discovered came from experienced technicians not having the manufacturer's training. So, one minimum requirement that must be met is that the technicians who work on your equipment must be factory-trained and certified. Does that sum it up?"*

Simms: *"Absolutely. I'm still amazed at the difference between using an experienced tech and a factory-trained certified tech. Now, once they have both certification and experience in our plant, they should save us even more time and money."*

Setting the Criteria with Questions

In setting the criteria, you often use a "generic" category or function of the feature, just as you did in the Orientation and Problem diagnosis questions.

"One criterion that would have to be met when selecting a supplier would be _____ (FAB). Is that about how you see it?"

"Another requirement you would like to see met is the supplier would _____ (FAB)?"

"One of the primary objectives you would want to accomplish when choosing suppliers would be ____ (FAB)?"

"So, based on the significance of the effects we've calculated, another requirement would be ____ (FAB)?"

"Are there any other criteria that need to be included in selecting this type of product?

Benefit Questions

When the prospect says "yes" to one of your criteria-setting questions, a belief has been established. This belief, based on irrefutable logic, is strong but open to being influenced by others (bosses, peers, competitor's salespeople, self).

The Benefit Questions lock in the criteria and lockout the competition. They help you and the prospect discover added values and other benefits the prospect will personally receive from using your product and service. This will, in turn, enhance the value the customer perceives they will receive from owning your product or service.

To ask a "Benefit Question" means asking the prospect about the benefits you can offer. You ask questions to determine the extent to which the customer believes they will benefit from what you sell.

By asking the Benefit Question and associating it with the criteria being set, you cause the buyer to:

1. **Build defenses:** Buyers are often challenged by themselves, their bosses, peers, and others about the justification for deciding to purchase a particular product or service or to change suppliers. Unless you help the buyer develop and practice defenses to support their buying decision, pressure from themselves and others may lead to a cancellation or stall.

2. **Prevent skepticism objections:** We, as Sales Professionals, often make claims about the benefits the customer will get. When we make spectacular claims, the buyer has no choice but to doubt us and require that we prove what we say. The person making the claims for benefits has the burden of proof.

3. **Know the most important benefits to the customer:** The benefits we tend to focus on are those that are important to us rather than the ones that are important to the customer. We can only know which benefits are essential to the customer when we ask them what they are.

4. Discover personal value: By asking the prospect to tell you the benefits they will receive, you discover the primary buying motives that help establish "personal" VALUE in the prospect's mind. Aside from the benefits they will tell you, there often will be highly personal benefits they won't tell you. Much of the information you gain here is related to the "subjective" value of your product/service.

5. Create attitudes: When you add emotion to a belief, you create an attitude. You may have successfully put a positive belief, such as a criterion, in place with the prospect. However, beliefs can be easily changed with new or credible contradictory information. But attitudes are very resistant to change - even in the face of new or credible contradictory information. You create attitudes by challenging the prospect with a challenging question of "WHY."

The "why" question causes people to defend their actions, statement, or position. The "why" question elicits the defense emotions. Challenging prospects with a "why" question causes them to generate and rehearse defenses for the action or decision. Doing this while with them enables you to support and reinforce the efforts.

A customer may believe what you offer will provide significant benefits, but beliefs are subject to change when presented with credible evidence to the contrary. Even getting challenged by someone else and not having any defense could cause the beliefs to change.

Attitudes, however, **are resistant to change** no matter how much credible evidence contrary to the original belief or behavior is presented. How does this happen?

Belief + Emotion = Attitude

Belief

You hold a belief to be valid until the information you receive causes you to change that belief. Beliefs are easy to change by providing new credible information.

Certain types of beliefs are easier to change into attitudes. These include:

- beliefs that were initially thought to be true without proof
- those that are subjective
- those that are arguably right when viewed from the perspective of specific experiences
- those that are connected to or supportive of some other substantial value

Emotion

An emotion is a feeling you get when you become aware of circumstances that have value to you.

Challenge

When you challenge a person's belief or behavior in a certain way, they can feel called upon to defend themselves.

Defense

Putting a person on the defensive evokes an emotion, which is then linked to the belief (or behavior). As noted earlier, you evoke the defense emotion by using the word or some form of the question, ***"WHY?"***

Attitude

An attitude is a belief that has an emotion attached to it. For our purposes in selling, we want that emotion to be defensive.

The more the belief (or behavior) is challenged, the stronger the attitude becomes.

Support – Challenge – Support: A good way to make this process highly effective is first to support the person's belief as you would when setting the criteria. Then challenge. And, finally, support their defense. That could be in the form of a headshake, a "me too," or even just a smile.

Attitudes – A Final Word: As you can tell, creating an attitude is straightforward. Ask yourself when you would usually ask the "WHY" question. When someone did something good or something bad (or simply something you disagreed with)? What type of attitude are you creating, good or bad? That said, the rule to follow is only to challenge beliefs and behaviors you want to see an increase in frequency and intensity.

To change an unintentional attitude, you, or someone else set, ask the person to help you with a problem you need to resolve. Ask them to argue favorably for the opposite point of view of the attitude you want to see weakened. Do this by continually challenging with some form of the "why" question. Do this gently at first. Another way is to catch them doing it the way you want to see repeated, and then, support – challenge – support.

Examples of Benefit Questions

- *"In addition to what we've discussed, what other value would you get by meeting your criteria?"*
- *"What other benefits do you see in having this function performed?"*
- *"How will the operational department benefit from having your criteria met?"*
- *"What additional value would your staff receive from having your criteria met?"*

For example:

Customer: *"This product seems to be of higher quality."*

Seller: *"I agree, and why do you say that?"*

Customer: *"Because it has _____ and _____!"*

Case Study: The Jill Ryan Scenario

The more you challenge them with questions, and the more you support their ability to respond (defend) successfully, the stronger the attitude becomes.

Since you've seen this scenario played out over the entire model so far, try to answer the "Benefit Questions" as they're asked below. Make it up.

F. 24-hour, 7-day service

A. available when you need service

B. less downtime

"In addition to what we've talked about, how else will the day shift benefit from having the equipment repaired for their shift?

"How will having access to service make the night supervisor feel?"

F telephone troubleshooting process

A. bring the right parts to call

B decrease downtime

"What benefits will accounting get from not having to log multiple trips for the same issue?"

"Why would the onsite maintenance benefit from this?"

F certified technicians

A know what to do

B reduces service time.

"How will this certification help with your project bidding for government contracts?"

"How would the sales department benefit?"

"Why would that be important to them?"

What happened when you started answering these Benefit Questions? What did it feel like when you just made something up? Do you think you could defend your made-up answers?

Just imagine what would happen if the 8-5 competitor now comes in. The customer says, *"We have to have 24/7 service.* "And the 8-5 competitor responds, *"We have low hourly rates; WHY do you want to spend that much for 24/7 service?* "Look out!

Your Case Study

Look at your USP FABs and develop Benefit Questions for them.

Summarize two or three FABs you practiced setting as criteria earlier and see if you can ask some Benefit Questions about them. For example, *"We talked about this FAB, that FAB, and the other FAB. What advantages do you see this package bringing to your department?"*

1. Write examples of how you would ask the Benefits Questions.

2. Think about the sales process you have been learning and predict the responses you might get.
3. Identify others in the organization who might benefit from your offer (others impacted by what you sell). This is one way to help the prospect see how they can become a "hero."

With the Benefit Questions tied directly to the criteria, we can get the prospective customer to defend the criteria, rehearse to sell internally, and make their claims about the benefits, thereby preventing skepticism-type objections and creating targeted favorable attitudes about our company, products/services, and ourselves.

Competitive Comparison Close

The Criteria/Benefit questions create the substance for a major closing strategy called the "Competitive Comparison Close." They enable the customer to clarify the capabilities necessary to solve the problems and provide the basis for a direct comparison with your competitors. Once your Unique Selling Points are in place as criteria for doing business, then the competitor, by default, is ruled out. Once the prospect has defended the criteria, the competitor is locked out.

Competitor Proof Your Current Customers

Ask your current customers what they like about the USPs they are receiving. Do this by first bringing up the capabilities you know are working well and putting a spotlight on them. Talk about them and then ask the Benefit Questions about them. Help your customer succeed in defending your light touch challenge. Continue to use this process on all your USP capabilities over multiple contacts. Over time, you will help them develop defenses to fend off your competitors and other internal challengers who might become champions for another supplier.

Summary

Setting your Unique Selling Points as minimum criteria to select a supplier weakens the competitor significantly. I've often reviewed Requests for Proposals (RFP) only to find that my competitors had influenced the criteria. However, in many cases, they did not know how to lock it in by challenging it, thereby creating an attitude that would be resistant to change by me or anyone else.

There are essentially three major sales strategies:

1. **Head-to-head.** This requires that you have at least a 3 to 1-advantage over the nearest competitor. Nowadays, even for the 500-pound gorilla, this is not the best primary strategy.
2. **Change the Rules to Change the Game.** This is what setting the Criteria does to the sales opportunity — once locked in place with the Benefit Questions, you truly have a game-changer.
3. **Piece of the Pie.** If you're getting knocked down by the 500-pound gorilla or your competitors have influenced the criteria to their favor, you may only be left with a "foot in the door" approach. Get some piece of the business, no matter how small. This is all you need to begin account penetration to get the opportunity to build relationships and consequently acquire the information you need, along with access to select critical audiences to run the P.R.O.S.P.E.C.T. Model to change the rules again.

9

Triggering Event Questions

Intent

The intent of the Triggering Event Questions category is to develop a win/win plan to achieve customer satisfaction.

Objectives

- Identify the next steps to advance the sale.
- Get the customer to see the steps necessary to do business with you mentally.
- Clarify the prospect company's logistical buying process.
- Initiate the process of determining who must do what, when, how, with what resources, in what time frame, and with what feedback loops occurring at what milestones.

Overview

The Triggering Events are a list of actions that must occur for the prospect to own your product/service. This implies that one step triggers the next, and consequently, step by step, you advance the sale.

Buying Process Logistics

- What is the next step?
- Who must do what, when, with what resources, and in what time frame?
- What is the sequence of events that will help us meet the ideal completion date?
- What is the best start date?
- Will Beta testing be required?
- How long will it take?
- Who will be involved?
- What are the milestones and measurements of success?
- What are the feedback loops?
- What will be needed in the follow-up process and account management plans?

Developing Triggering Event Questions

Triggering Events become part of your call objectives. They help you with the strategic planning process. "Just calling to set up a meeting to meet and get to know you" or "Just calling to follow up" are not strong enough call objectives to justify the expense of that call.

You must have your call objectives predefined. Know what steps must be done or the sale will fail, and then add any steps based on the specifics of each sales opportunity.

Be prepared with the NEXT STEPS necessary to move the sale forward, independent of whether or not the prospect completed the action item you are following up on. These steps will be augmented by the customer's buying process and action items that need to be taken care of each specific sales opportunity.

Steps in the Sales Process

Several years ago, several Fortune 500 companies went through an exercise at their annual sales meetings in which they asked the salespeople how they knew they were 25%, then 50%, then 75% of the way to closing a sale. What milestones had they reached that gave them that level of confidence that the sale would close? The percentages represent the probability that the sale will be won when that milestone is achieved.

The percentages and milestones below are based on the Strategic Sales Plan's logic. Review this plan and determine if you need that step or not. You can make those determinations by identifying the consequences of not doing each of them. Cross off, add, or modify the list as needed.

Once you validate your sales process steps, you can then establish what's within each milestone for what you sell.

The goal is to have mutually agreed-upon percentages for each milestone based on the steps completed in your sales process. Now, when you say you've got a 50% chance of winning the sale, you will know that steps 1-25 are complete.

Percent / Milestone / Steps Completed

10% Profile and Qualify the Sales Prospect (Steps 1-8)
20% Research the Prospect's Needs (Steps 9-12)
30% Conduct the Competitor Analysis (Steps 13-16)
50% Establish the Value of What You Sell (Steps 17-25)
70% Complete the Logistics Steps (Steps 26-32)
80% Propose, Present, and Negotiate (Steps 33-39)
90% Deliver Your Products & Services (Steps 40-42)
100% Manage Your Account (Steps 43-44)

Strategic Sales Plan

Profile & Qualify the Sales Prospect

1. Compare the prospect with the profile of your most desirable customers.
2. Identify decision-makers.
3. Identify the initial people to contact.
4. Select and sequence methods of contact.
5. Set call objectives.
6. Make contact.
7. Establish trust and rapport.
8. Qualify the prospect for the current sales opportunity. **GO/NO GO**

Research the Prospect's Needs

1. Research the prospect's products, services, and company.
2. Research prospect's critical processes.
3. Research prospect's business plans.
4. Identify potential for your other products and services.

Conduct the Competitor Analyses

1. Identify your external and internal competitors.
2. Conduct competitor analyses.
3. Update your list of Unique Selling Points.
4. Identify potential objections. **GO/NO GO**

Establish the Value of What You Sell

1. Neutralize, prevent, preempt, and respond to potential objections.
2. Focus the topics of conversation on your Unique Selling Points (USPs).
3. Identify the signs caused by your USPs' missing Advantages and Benefits.
4. Confirm the problems caused by the missing USPs.

5. Quantify the costs of not having your USPs to establish the value of the solution.
6. Set your USPs as specifications that must be met to solve the problems.
7. Competitor Proof with Benefits Questions.
8. Complete the interviews with key decision-makers. **GO/NO GO**
9. Validate any cost-benefit data that used industry standards.

Complete the Logistics Steps

1. Advise and get agreement on "Next Steps" to advance the sale.
2. Outline feedback loops, milestones, measurements, and follow-up process.
3. Develop product/service delivery phase-in plans.
4. Determine product/service availability. **GO/NO GO**
5. Complete required pre-purchase approvals. **GO/NO GO**
6. Exchange any additional data, specifications, or financial information.
7. Identify and prepare Recommenders to be your champions.

Propose, Present, and Negotiate

1. Prepare and submit the Customer Value Proposition (CVP).
2. Conduct sales presentation using the CVP format.
3. Prospect affirms your ability to meet criteria. **GO/NO GO**
4. Conclude final negotiations.
5. Final budget approval received. **GO/NO GO**
6. The contract is signed, or the letter of engagement is received.
7. Customer notifies the current supplier(s).

Deliver Your Products & Services

1. Identify and arrange to meet any critical "support people."
2. Identify specific End Users involved in the project.
3. Conduct quality checks of the product and service delivery.

Manage Your Account

1. Implement sales activities to competitor-proof and grow the account.
2. Know the signs your account is in trouble before it's too late.

Examples of Triggering Events Questions

- *"I guess the next step would be for me to demonstrate how we can meet your criteria."*
- *"What would be the process for us to get the opportunity to demonstrate our ability to meet your criteria?"*
- *"What additional information do you need for us to continue the process?"*
- *"Can you issue a purchase order for the trial?"*
- *"What is the next step to move the process forward? What would be the time frame?"*
- *"Who else would need to be involved in the process?"*
- *"Who in your organization will need to receive this information?"*
- *"I guess my next step would be to review how we can meet your expectations. When you feel comfortable with our plan, I will double-check our inventory to ensure we meet your needs."*
- *"If you would check on your inventory levels, that would help us do the math when we get back together. What else do you see we need to accomplish?"*

Case Study: The Jill Ryan Scenario

In the previous module, Jill set three criteria to rule out the competition effectively. Her prospect, Mr. Simms, successfully defended the criteria when Jill asked him the Benefit Questions.

Since Mr. Simms is the Final Authority, she could easily present her case and ask for the order at this meeting. However, Jill wants to ensure that when she gets the business, she keeps it.

For this example, I've used one of the strategies (Interim Action Plan) discussed below to help power up this step.

Ryan: *"Mr. Simms, as I see it, my next step would be briefly describing how our company can meet your criteria. Then, I would like to set up meetings with your maintenance supervisors to review the types of repair service calls they most frequently make so that we might propose ways of preventing some of the problems. What else do you see we need to do before I develop a proposal?"*

Simms: *"I need to verify the numbers we discussed just to be sure we're on target."*

Ryan: *"Yes, good idea. When we get together, who else would you want to have present for the discussion?"*

Simms: *"I'm going to call our onsite maintenance manager, the morning shift person, and the night shift supervisor to see if we can schedule the meeting for the time the shift takes place."*

Ryan: *"All right, let's go ahead and schedule that now so that your people will have ample notice. Let's reserve a couple of optional dates to choose from. What works better for you and your staff?"*

Simms: *"Let's look at 7:00 AM on Monday next week to get the information from the weekend crew. If that doesn't work, let's look at mid-next week, say Wednesday at the same time."*

Ryan: *"I should have the draft proposal back to you by Thursday this week so we can highlight what we need to verify at the meetings."*

Simms: *"Sounds good. I'll let you know when we all confirm for the meeting."*

Power Up the Triggering Events Step

The Triggering Events are, by default, a major closing strategy called the "Next Step Close." To power it up, you can use other structures within the same family of closes. Close on the next steps to advance your sale with the following:

- Next Step or Plan of Action Close
- Agenda Close
- Interim Action Plan Close
- Show Them How to Own Close

Next Step or Plan of Action Close

List the steps both you and the buyer must do to advance the sale. This is the standard Triggering Events closing strategy. For most sales situations, it is powerful enough just as it is.

In the "Next Step" or "Plan of Action" closing strategy, you always keep your customer informed about the next steps in the process. Ask them what additional steps they feel need to be taken.

Strategy: End each meeting with an agreement on the next steps. For example:

"I guess my next step would be to review how we can meet your expectations. When you feel comfortable with our plan, I would like to double-check our inventory to ensure we can meet your needs."

"If you would check on your inventory levels, that would help us do the math when we get back together. What else do you see we need to accomplish?"

Now, ask yourself if it would be stronger if you closed this meeting by setting your next meeting so you both had "deadlines" to complete the action items. How about sending an e-mail structured as the Interim Action Plan or a text with the agreed-upon action items and due dates? Could pre-closing some critical agenda items also be worth adding them to the e-mail or text?

Remember, many companies operate under the International Standards Organization (ISO) guidelines for quality, which requires documented agreed-upon action items and follow-up. Some organizations also require that scheduled meetings have a printable agenda for the record.

Think about a current sale you are in the process of making. What are the next steps? Where are those next steps in your list of steps in your sales process?

Agenda Close

This is a method to pre-close your action plan for the meeting. You do this by stating the agenda for the contact or meeting (phone or in-person).

Strategy: Begin each meeting with agreement on the agenda. If the prospect agrees to the action items on the agenda, they are, in effect, agreeing to move forward. When the prospect says, "Okay, let's get started," you have just pre-closed on several steps in your sales process. For example:

"First, I would like to give you a brief overview of our company to help orient and define some of our capabilities. Then, if I could get some information about your organization to quickly determine if there is an area where we can help you..." (state areas of Unique Selling Points as they relate to the four business needs.)

"After that, we can review ways we offer solutions based on cost-effectiveness. How does that agenda sound?"

Personally, I prefer to send the agenda ahead of a meeting that I've set. That way, the start and stop times and what we'll accomplish during the meeting are defined. The Interim Action Plan closing strategy keeps the ball rolling between meetings.

Interim Action Plan Close

Blocks the competition between calls and commits the prospect.

The Interim Action Plan is designed to keep the prospect involved between meetings. It can be written during or at the end of the meeting. It can be sent in an e-mail or as an attachment. If brief, it can be sent in a text, which can then be exported to print as many companies require.

The process lists the action items that should be completed between meetings. Casually and conversationally, identify who will do each one and how long it will take to complete them so you can set the next meeting. If you know other decision-makers will need to be involved, bring that up and make sure you get their names spelled correctly, their roles identified, and their contact information.

Example: Sales rep Bob and Customer Joe.

Interim Action Plan

Customer Name / Your Company Name

Current Date

Joe 1 - Determine the number of new containers needed and e-mail Bob with size requirements.

Bob 2 - Confirm inventory availability.

Joe 3 - Meet with engineers to find out when they plan to move the rusted steel drums and see if one of Bob's plastic drums could be used to test it.

Joe 4 - Arrange for engineering staff to be at the next meeting to discuss specification requirements.

NEXT MEETING

Date / Time: June 15, 2007, from 3 PM to 4:30 PM

Location: Customer Company, central conference room

Participants: Bob, Joe, and engineering staff person (Joe to advise)

Notes about this brief IAP:

- The Interim Action Plan can be used not only during the account acquisition process but also to monitor performance, provide feedback, and prevent the competition from moving in.
- The Interim Action Plan can be used after any prospect or client/customer meeting in which two or more action items are assigned.
- Include an item that will get done during this meeting so that you can mark it as complete.
- The list should begin with an action item the salesperson would do.
- If possible, the plan should include an action item for the prospect to complete that's quick and easy to do.

Think about all that you've accomplished with this simple Interim Action Plan closing strategy:

- Provide a written plan with action items listed and timelines for both the customer and seller to accomplish between meetings.
- Demonstrate, in writing, your commitment to do what you say you are going to do.
- Get a commitment, in writing, from your prospect to carry out the action items that would advance the sale.
- Set it so you can monitor and document the account's activities to ensure the buyer and seller fulfill the requirements.

- Have a guide to monitor and document performance against the sales plan.
- Demonstrate organization and clear direction to advancing the sale.
- Block the competition between sales calls and ensure that a next step and a follow-up date are set before leaving the prospect. You have your next appointment!
- Weakened current competitor's position.

Interim Action Plan Practice - Think about the last prospect you talked with and where you left with action items to do. Did the prospect have action items as well? Remember, engage the prospect to get them to help carry out those steps in the sales/buying process that they can do. Write an Interim Action Plan based on the last prospect where you both have action items.

Show Them How to Own Close

Walks a new buyer through the steps of how to buy from you.

This close assumes that not all of your prospects will know how to own your product or service. Do you know what paperwork and fees are necessary to buy a consultant's services, a piece of real estate, a car, a business, a vacuum cleaner, a computer, or any product or service on the market?

In each instance, you depend on the salesperson to know which forms to complete and where to file them, don't you? How are you going to pay for it? Do you know every company's terms for payment? Probably not. You're not expected to, and neither is your prospect. To use this close, simply state the buying process for your particular product or service:

"To own this, ...we will need to _____ (State your process)."

"To acquire the franchise for this area, you will need to be able to store the products in a low-humidity environment. What storage facilities do you have available?"

The less someone understands how to do something important, the higher their anxiety. Therefore, be prepared for baby steps or risk causing cold feet and running off the prospect.

Developing Your Triggering Event Questions

You have several call objectives to accomplish during your initial contact with a prospective customer after discovering their needs and before you end the meeting. Review the Strategic Sales Plan list of sales process steps provided earlier in this chapter and identify which items, as well as any others specific to your product/service, you would typically accomplish after discovering needs. These become your next steps or Triggering Events.

List five call objectives you want to accomplish with the prospective customer you're using to build your case study.

Next, identify and list the action items that would advance your sale if they could be completed between your meetings with this prospect. Be sure to include at least one for the prospect to do.

Summary

Building a checklist of all the steps and sub-steps in your sales process is the best way to ensure you don't miss any that might jeopardize the sale. Use this list of steps in your pre-call planning and post-call review, and go back into pre-call planning for the next call. Use it to itemize your Agenda for the next meeting and to help with your Interim Action Plan.

10

Customer Value Proposition

Intent

The intent of the Customer Value Proposition (CVP) is to use irrefutable logic to confirm your ability to meet the criteria established during the P.R.O.S.P.E.C.T. interview.

Objectives

- Understand the strategy underlying the "Situational
- Analysis" phase of the presentation.
- Learn how to prevent stalls by demonstrating the seriousness of the problem with the prospect's facts and figures.
- List and get agreement on the criteria upon which the customer will base their buying decision.
- Use irrefutable logic to confirm how your company can meet the criteria.
- Demonstrate a financial win/win transaction for buyer and seller.
- Initiate the plan of action.

Overview

At this stage in the process, you are about to present and confirm how your company can meet the criteria established during the sales interview.

Customer-focused presentations that directly address their Criteria are more effective than the "tell them everything" shotgun approach.

When the presentation also includes a cost-benefit analysis, it becomes a "Customer Value Proposition (CVP)" or a "Value Improvement Proposition (VIP)."

The presentation will consist of five steps. The information necessary to use this highly effective presentation method comes from conducting the strategically designed P.R.O.S.P.E.C.T. interview.

The primary thrust of this process is to confirm your ability to meet the prospect's criteria and to lay out a plan of action to implement your solutions.

Steps in the Customer Value Proposition

The Customer Value Proposition uses the information you've gathered during your interviews. When you complete the CVP, you can be assured that you've completed many of the most critical steps in the sales process.

1. **Situational Analysis:** Present your understanding of the situation to establish trust and rapport.
2. **Economic and Other Impact:** Quantify the seriousness of the problems to build and sustain motivation.
3. **Selection Criteria and Capabilities:** List the criteria for selecting a solution and state how you meet them.
4. **Investment and Financial Comparison Analysis:** Present a balanced financial comparison.
5. **Plan for Implementation:** Discuss your plan of action to deliver the products/services

Step 1. Situational Analysis

Summarize your understanding of the situation and challenges faced by the customer. The more you demonstrate to the customer that you genuinely understand the situation, the more they trust that your solutions will be on target. This will help you establish the power of Psychological Truth.

Psychological Truth: Create a psychological obligation to understand you.

If you sincerely try to understand another person's point of view, they become psychologically obligated to try to understand your point of view.

The information for this step comes primarily from the Profile, Research, Orientation, Symptom, and Problem Questions.

Case Study: The Jill Ryan Scenario

Jill: *"As a result of the meetings with Mr. Simms, Mr. Jacobs, and Mrs. Peterson, I have developed an analysis of the current situation. From the data we collectively put together, it looks as though conveyor systems #3 and #5, which are used for the initial processing, receive three times the number of wash downs as the other systems. They also show the highest number of service calls for repair.*

"Actual repair time is taking a little longer than it should because rather than using factory-recommended troubleshooting procedures, the technicians are changing out parts until they can find the real problem. This practice tends to aggravate the need to return to the shop to get the necessary additional parts."

Your Case Study

Using the prospective customer you chose to work with, briefly define your understanding of your prospect's situation.

Begin with the Profile and Research information to provide a general overview. Then, orient to an area, describe the symptoms, and define the problem. Repeat this process for each problem uncovered that you can support with symptoms.

It is essential to write this information down, or you will often find yourself doubting what you are saying.

Step 2. Economic and Other Impacts

Discuss the seriousness of the problems using the information you acquired during your Effects and Consequences questions. Emphasize those problems you can resolve with your Unique Selling Points. Include the associated costs (financial, subjective, and emotional) to the customer of not having the advantages and benefits provided by you (and your product/service, company).

Emphasizing the economic, emotional, and subjective impact of the issues helps create the business case for the proposed change. If this area isn't vital and there is no other powerful motivation, such as a top-down high-priority Strategic Initiative in place, the project will probably be stalled, cut during the routine budget reviews, or become a commodity bid type purchase.

You can display this information in tables, bullet points, or other representations highlighting your business case for moving forward.

Case Study: The Jill Ryan Scenario

Jill: The problems uncovered in three areas produced operational use costs not accounted for in the service contract but clearly being paid out of currently budgeted dollars.

These areas are 1) the number of breakdowns per shift, 2) the amount of time spent waiting for the repair service, and 3) the percentage of parts damaged as a result of not using factory-certified technicians (estimated at 10% of total parts costs).

Additionally, with limited storage capacity and many customers using "just in time" delivery, lengthy breakdowns can severely impact customer relations. So far this year, the company has not lost any customers; however, the marketing team has had to make some concessions to keep two of your medium-sized customers.

The monthly breakdown is as follows:

Monthly Costs

Price to get

Ten service calls at $80.00 each = $800

Use and Hidden Costs

After-hours breakdown down (wait) time costs = $2,250

Drive time to get extra parts = $500

Parts (including damaged parts) = $400

Total Repair Service Costs (Get + Use for all department budgets) = $3,950

ANNUAL BUDGET (Use Costs) $3,150 X 12 Months = $37,800

Your Case Study

Based on the current prospect you are working with, quantify any hidden costs to the prospect because they do not have the advantages and benefits of your unique selling points.

Step 3. Selection Criteria/Capabilities

Opening Remarks could include: "In the following chart, the critical issues that need to be addressed by our product/service are on the left, and our capability to provide is on the right."

Use the terms the prospect uses. For example, Criteria, Specifications, Expectations, Objectives, Requirements, Conditions, Standards, etc. It's a game-changer if your Unique Selling Points (USPs) are included in the list of specifications. If not, work your USPs into how you will meet their criteria.

Recommended Selection Criteria: You can add recommended specifications that include your Unique Selling Points and items they truly need to make the project work. These add to your trust levels.

For example, "...during our analysis and our understanding of the goals for the project, we suggest the following additional requirements (expectations, etc.) be added to your specifications document."

Your solutions will now fit the defined and agreed-upon criteria. State the features from which the requirements have been developed and set. Use the advantages and benefits to clarify how the feature will irrefutably reduce or eliminate the effects/ consequences.

Be clear that this section includes the criteria you set and the specifications set by the customer. Locate your criteria next to the related customer specifications.

Note that if you are up against known competitors, you may have to emphasize the need for the criteria to be met, or the results will not be forthcoming, and the consequences will occur.

Case Study: The Jill Ryan Scenario

Ordinarily, this section is displayed in a side-by-side listing. In the left-hand column, under the heading of "Criteria for Selecting a Supplier," you would list each of the prospect's specifications intermingled with each of the Criteria you set in place.

Across from each specification or criteria under the heading of "Your Company Meets the Criteria," you would discuss how you can meet it. In the presentation below, I will list the criteria and, under it, discuss how it is met for the Jill Ryan Scenario.

1. Open 24 hours, seven days per week

Our company maintains a staff of technicians at our facility 24 hours, seven days per week. This eliminates after-hours surcharges and, more importantly, eliminates downtime in excess of expected travel and repair time.

2. Telephone diagnostic process

The dispatchers are technicians on rotation. They use a quick standardized questionnaire to narrow down the diagnosis before they leave the shop. This troubleshooting procedure, developed in conjunction with the factory and years of experience, enables the technicians to select the right parts to minimize having to return to get the correct parts.

3. Factory certified technicians

All technicians are certified by the factory to troubleshoot, diagnose, and repair problems quickly. This also ensures that they know how to make the repairs in such a manner as to avoid accidentally breaking parts.

Your Case Study

How You Meet the Criteria: List your prospect's specifications and the criteria you set to select a solution in the left-hand column. Across from it, in the right-hand column, describe how you will meet the requirements. Do this by stating the feature and explaining how this feature will eliminate the effects/consequences by describing the advantages and benefits.

Step 4. Investment and Financial Comparison Analysis

Opening remarks could include: "Based on the needs identified and matched with our company's capabilities, we can show both short- and longer-term cost-effective delivery of solutions that meet your expectations.

List Style Presentation: List each item. Next to it, write the cost.

Balance Sheet Style Presentation: This is a compelling way to provide a comparison if you have the numbers available. If not, then leave the competitor and the difference columns blank. Let the customer fill them in. In the "additional use costs" area, include what happens when the customer doesn't have the Advantages and Benefits of your Unique Selling Points' Features.

In the first set of rows, include the line items and cost.

Note that if you don't have the competition's numbers (costs), you can add a column and leave it blank for the prospect to complete.

In the next set of rows, list the additional costs associated with using your product/service versus the competitor's products/services.

In the next set of rows, calculate the projected costs. Use the product's expected life or the service agreement's length.

Heading: Line-Item Costs (Items and costs)

1. First item and cost – in the second column, write your competitors.
2. Second item and cost – in the second column, write your competitors.
3. Continue as needed – in the second column, write your competitors.

Total Line-Item Costs – in the second column, total your competitors.

Heading: Additional Use Costs:

1. First, list the additional item and cost – in the second column, write your competitors.
2. Second, list the additional item and cost – in the second column, write your competitors.
3. Continue as needed

Total Additional Use Costs (yours and the competitors)

Heading: Projected cost savings (or projected unaccounted-for additional use costs)

Now calculate the additional use costs projected over the product's life or the service agreement's length.

Competitive Equivalency Comparison: This strategy is an option to using the entire balance sheet illustrated above. Here, you can make statements to equalize pricing or other issues. For example, if you can double throughput or your product is shipped 8 to a case, and the competitor ships 6 to a case, these differences must be displayed in the proposal.

State the areas of difference and then balance out the differences to get an apple-to-apple comparison.

Case Study: The Jill Ryan Scenario

The representation below is very similar to the one developed and used as an example during the Effects/Consequences Questions. During the Customer Value Proposition, you can show both sides (their costs versus your costs).

Monthly Total Budget Impact (using actual current expenditures)

Ten service calls per month = $800 after-hours breakdown versus $1,250 for Ryan's company

Waiting costs = $2,250 versus $ 0.00 for Ryan's company.

Excess drive time to get parts = $500 versus $250 for Ryan's company

Extra parts (includes damaged parts) = $400 versus $364 for Ryan's company

Total Price to Get + Cost to Use = $4,036 versus $1,864 for Ryan's company

Annualized Total Budget Impact (using actual budgeted expenditures)

Cost to Use = $3,150 versus $614 for Ryan's company

X 12-month contract = $37,800 versus $7,368 for Ryan's company

+ Price to Get (12 months) $9,600 versus $15,000 for Ryan's company

= Bottom Line Impact = $47,400 versus $22,368 for Ryan's company

Your Case Study

As you can see from the Jill Ryan example, it will be very difficult for the Final Authority (person responsible for all budgets impacted) to say, "I can get it from your competitor for a lot less." Remember, these are the prospect's facts and figures, not Jill's or, in this case, yours.

Set this up in as many columns and rows as you need.

Quick Question: What if you don't know the competitor's pricing structure? Provide yours and leave the column for the competitor blank. Just ensure the prospect has the formulas to arrive at the figures themselves.

Step 5. Plan for Implementation

Opening remarks can include: "The following list of action items is provided to map out the key steps necessary to advance the project under consideration."

Describe each step necessary to implement the solution. When possible, within the first seven steps, **one early step should already be completed**, and **another step following that should be in progress. It will be achieved without the prospect's "okay," another step should include a feedback loop for** the designated people. Dates should be associated with events and dates on the calendar.

The psychology behind this strategy is that half the population has a personality characteristic in which the preference is to "go with the flow," not to make decisions but to hunger for information (feedback). They also are "event" schedulers, first of the month, end of the day, etc., rather than date and time schedulers.

What you've done is set up a flow that will occur without any decisions made by the prospect. You've also put in a step that feeds their need to know. Finally, you put them in a position where they have to decide (which they don't like to do) to "stop the sale" and shut off the flow and the information rather than putting them in the position to decide to start the sale. If you associate the dates with events, you give them something they can understand.

Okay, that's fine, but what about the other half of the decision-makers? How will they like this strategy? Well, that's easy. The other half are people who like to plan, schedule, and organize. They like making decisions and being assured that the plan is detailed and that they can understand and believe it will work. So, as you can see, this family of closing strategies we discussed earlier (Triggering Events) will work consistently with both ends of the continuum for this personality characteristic.

Within the plan, include actions and items such as who will do what, in what sequence, with what resources, milestones, measurements, feedback loops, follow-up plans, and the ideal starting date tied to an event.

Case Study: The Jill Ryan Scenario

Again, this is best constructed in a two-column table with the Action Item listed and next to it the "Progress to Date." Below, I will present the Action Item and, beneath it, the Progress.

Action Item 1: Identify hidden and collateral costs associated with the current methods of procuring motor controller repair service.

Progress: Completed and included in this report.

Action Item 2: Present a Proposal to minimize excessive costs.

Progress: Completed and included in this report.

Action Item 3: Develop a monthly tracking system to monitor progress to minimize excessive costs. Monthly feedback will be sent to Mr. Simms, Mr. Jacobs, and each shift supervisor.

Progress: Our company is preparing standard forms to fit within your system. To be completed by mid-month.

Action Item 4: Complete the requisition order.

Progress: Purchasing will complete the order upon approval from your team.

Action Item 5: Notify current supplier (30 days required)

Progress: Purchasing to notify.

Note: This process will now continue with any additional information that is to be included.

Your Case Study

Present Your Plan of Action: Review the steps you developed for your sales process during the Triggering Events Questions and the Interim Action Plan phases of your sales process. List the standard steps you anticipate using with the prospect for your spreadsheet learning process.

Remember, the Customer Value Proposition is designed to foster an attitude and atmosphere of a business transaction in process. By using the information gained during the diagnostic interview, the presentation to confirm your ability to meet the prospective customer's criteria will be on target.

Again, it would be best to present this information in a two-column table.

Interim Action Plan

After concluding your presentation, be prepared to write an Interim Action Plan to advance the sale continually.

Summary

The Customer Value Proposition gains its power by establishing rapport, showing the costs of the problems (some of which only you can solve with your USPs), showing side-by-side the criteria and how they can be met, by showing the financial plan, and by laying out a plan to move forward.

Understand that unless you ask the P.R.O.S.P.E.C.T. Model questions, you can't write the Customer Value Proposition. I'm just saying you have to ask the questions!

11

Review

Intent

The intent of this chapter is to increase your comfort level with using the Value Selling Strategies P.R.O.S.P.E.C.T. Model in a conversation.

Objectives

- Review P.R.O.S.P.E.C.T. & FAB formula
- Review intent and example questions
- Learn to combine questions

Overview

We have now worked through each of the components of the P.R.O.S.P.E.C.T. Model.

Recall that to use the model, it is necessary to understand how it is connected to the features, advantages, and benefits of your product, service, company, and self.

The Profile, Research, and Triggering Events Questions provide you with the information you need to plan the sales process.

Answer: Feature, Advantage, or Benefit for each question:

- What do you use to orient the prospect?
- Where do the symptoms come from?
- What do you use to diagnose the problem?
- What do you quantify?
- What do you set as criteria?

Check Answers: 1) F, 2) missing A&B, 3) missing F, 4) cost of not having the A & B, 5) F supported with A & B.

Conduct the Sales Interview

P.R.O.S.P.E.C.T. Model Interviewing Strategy

Conducting the Sales Interview with the P.R.O.S.P.E.C.T. Model would follow the pattern of asking each of the questions so that the intent of the question is fulfilled. You know if the intent is met by the responses you get. If you do not get the desired response, then you must re-ask the question until it is clear that the intent has been achieved.

The **P** stands for **Profile.** The intent of the Profile Questions is to qualify the prospect and identify the buying influences.

- *"What size is your operation?"*
- *"Aside from yourself, who else would be involved in making the decisions about buying?"*

The **R** stands for **Research.** The intent of the Research Questions is to gain customer and competitor information to develop a win/win sales strategy.

- *"What does your organization do to make money?"*
- *"What is your end product?"*
- *"How do you currently ____?"*

- *"What are the critical steps in the process?"*
- *"Is this a growing area for you?"*
- *"Who do you sell to?"*
- *"Who are your current suppliers?"*

The **O** stands for **Orientation.** The intent of the Orientation Questions is to focus the conversation on areas where you are strong, the competitor is weak, and the customer has needs.

- *"Let's focus for a moment in the area of ...?" Then simply state an area where you have unique selling points, an area where you are strong, and your competitor is weak.*
- *"Based on what we've been talking about, there are three areas that raise questions. The first is _____. The second is ____. And the third is _____. Which of these do you want to talk about first?"*
- *"What would make that more profitable for you?"*

The **S** stands for **Symptom.** The intent of the Symptom Questions is to identify both the obvious and the hidden needs not being met by the competitor.

"Looking closely at _____, what are your greatest areas of concern?" Then, name specific items that are your competitor's weaknesses where you have strengths, but never name the competitor. These are what you would see when the prospect does NOT have the advantages and benefits of your USPs features.

- *"Where's the pain?"*
- *"What gives you the most headaches?"*
- *"Where do you invest the most time?"*
- *"What would make it better for you?"*

The second **P** stands for **Problem.** The intent of the Problem Questions is to define the root causes of the symptoms and confirm the existence of problems.

- *"That points to a problem, doesn't it?"*
- *"If you're having _____ and ____, then that points to a problem with not having____, doesn't it?"*
- *"What do you think is causing that problem?"*
- *"That could be a problem"* (continue to ask an Effects question).

The **E** stands for both **Effects** and **Consequences.** This set of questions is also denoted as **E/C** or **E/c.** The intent of the Effects Questions is to quantify the seriousness of the problem to establish the value of the solution. The Consequences part of the question determines what it will cost in the future if the problem is not solved.

- *"What effect does that have on your current budget?"*
- *"How often does that happen?"*
- *"What does it cost each time it happens?"*
- *"What would you think the potential costs would be if that problem occurred?"*
- *"What will it cost over the next year if the problem is not solved?"*

The Effects/Consequences, when displayed in a "T" format, becomes a major closing strategy known as the "Comparison Balance Sheet Close."

The **C** stands for both the **Criteria** and the **Benefits** Questions. This set of questions is also denoted as **C/B** or **C/b.** The intent of the Criteria Questions is to get agreement on the criteria that must be met to select a solution.

These criteria will include your Unique Selling Points (USP) to weaken the competitor's position or rule them out entirely.

When you state the advantages and benefits to explain how the USP's feature will reduce or eliminate the symptoms and effects/consequences, then you have established "irrefutable logic."

For example, in setting the criteria, you might summarize your discussion to this point by saying,

- *"So, one of your criteria for selecting a supplier would be _____."* (Now state your feature by the function it serves and further explains it with its advantages and benefits, which will reduce or eliminate the effects and consequences).

- Another example would be, *"Then one of the requirements that would have to be met would be____."* Again, state your feature by the function it serves and use the advantages and benefits to clarify how it will be done.
- *"So, one Criteria that would have to be met for you to consider changing suppliers would be_____ (FAB). Is that pretty much how you see it?"*

The **Benefits** part of the question gets the customer to ***rehearse a defense*** of the criteria using their own words. This helps prepare them to ***sell internally for you*** when you're not around or sell to people you have difficulty reaching. It helps them create ***positive attitudes*** about your products/services. They empower the ***prospect to make the claims about benefits rather than you***. This ***prevents skepticism-type objections***. They help you to ***discover the personal value*** that would motivate the customer.

- *"In addition to what we've talked about, what other advantages would you get from having your criteria met?"*
- *"Who else would benefit from this?"*
- *"What other benefits would the accounting department get?"*
- *"What other value would you get from having these criteria met?"*
- *"What additional value would you get by having your Criteria met?"*

The Criteria/Benefits questions are the substance of a major closing strategy known as the "Competitive Comparison Close."

The **T** stands for **Triggering Events**. The intent of the Triggering Events Questions is to help you and the prospect develop a win/win plan of action to achieve customer satisfaction and to get the customer to mentally walk through the steps necessary to do business with you.

- *"I guess my next step would be to demonstrate how our company can meet your criteria."*

- *"Then, the next step would be for me to meet with the engineering manager."*
- *"Then we'll need to set up a schedule for a beta test."*
- *"After that, what do you see as our next step?"*

The **Triggering Events** questions are based on a family of "Next Step" style closes, including the "Agenda Close," the "Ownership Question Close," and the "Plan of Action Close.

Memory Work: Commit to memory, generic questions you can use comfortably so that no matter where you are in the process, you can come up with the next set of questions and simply "fill in the blanks" with your FABs.

Combining Questions and Going Ballistic!

Ensuring that the **intent of the question** is met, how the question is asked, or in what sequence now takes on a lesser role. Combining questions or re-sequencing them to better match the flow of the conversation is not only permissible but is emphatically encouraged.

Most of the questions in the P.R.O.S.P.E.C.T. Model can be used in various combinations. They can also be asked in any sequence except for the Criteria/Benefit Questions.

Recall that Benefit Questions should only be asked when linked directly with one or more criteria. The ability to re-sequence the questions is essential if this is going to be a conversation with the prospect.

Let's quickly review examples of how the questions are combined and re-sequenced. We will use the Jill Ryan case study scenario as an example of the formats provided.

Combination Examples using the Jill Ryan Scenario

Orientation question and Symptom question:

Generic: *"When thinking about the specific process you are currently using, what are your greatest areas of concern?"*

Specific: *"In thinking about after-hour or weekend breakdowns, what are your greatest areas of concern?"*

Combine and reverse the sequence of the Orientation and Symptom questions:

Generic: *"What are your greatest concerns with the process you are currently using?"*

Specific: *"What are your greatest concerns with the after-hour and weekend emergency call process you currently use?"*

Combine the Orientation, Symptom, and Effects questions:

Generic: *"In looking at the current process, how often do you have to respond* to (now state the specific item)?"

Specific: "*In looking at the current system, how long does it take to get someone out here?"*

Combine the Problem and Effect questions:

Generic: *"That could be a problem with* (now state the diagnoses but don't pause, rather continue with). *How often do you see that occur?"*

Specific: *"That could be a problem with tracking down a repair technician. How often do you see that occurring?"*

Combine the Problem, Criteria, and Effects questions:

Generic: *"That points to a problem with* (state the diagnosis or missing feature's function, but don't pause), *so one of your criteria would be to _____.* (now state the function of the feature, the advantages, and benefits; don't pause and say) *how often does that happen?"*

Specific: "*That points to a problem with hours the technicians work, so one of your criteria would have to include selecting a supplier that has the same hours of operation you do so that they would be available when you need them and you would not have excessive downtime waiting on a repair technician, how often do you have to call for emergency help after hours?"*

Combine the Triggering Events and Profile questions:

Generic: *"I guess our next step would be to schedule a meeting to explore this further. Who else from your company would you want to invite to this meeting?"*

Specific: *"I guess our next step would be to schedule a meeting to explore this further. Who else from your company would you want to invite to this meeting?"*

Combine the Consequences and Criteria questions:

Generic: *"So if we are going to prevent that problem from impacting your budget for the rest of this year, an important objective we'll want to achieve with this program is to include a* (now state your Feature, and explain it with its Advantage and Benefit then add), *make sense?"*

Specific: *"So if we are going to prevent that problem from impacting your budget for the rest of this year, an important objective we'll want to achieve with this service is to include a provision that only certified technicians be sent to service the equipment which would then reduce the service call time and parts breakage, thereby lowering your costs."*

To go ballistic with combining questions, you must first clearly **understand the intent of each question type**. The caution is to ensure that each question's intent is accomplished, or you risk diluting the power of this model. Stay flexible, and roll with the conversation. Just ensure that the intent of each question is accomplished.

To "Ask" Or "Not Ask" The Questions

What happens if you do not ask?

- Profile Questions
- Research Questions

- Orientation Questions
- Symptom Questions
- Problem Questions
- Effects/Consequence Questions
- Criteria Benefits Questions
- Triggering Events Questions

Customer Value Proposition

The Customer Value Proposition uses the information you've gathered during your interview and enables you to:

1. **Present your understanding of the situation**. This is based on the information gained during the Profile, Research, Orientation, Symptom, and Problem Questions. It establishes your right to be heard as someone who understands their situation.

2. **Quantify the seriousness of the problems.** This was developed with the Effects/Consequences Questions. It shows that they are indeed leaking money, and that helps create a sense of urgency to continue. If dollar figures aren't available, rely on subjective values.

3. **Present your solutions and compare them against the criteria.** The criteria were developed during the Criteria/Benefits Questions. These include both the prospect's defined specifications and the criteria you were able to set that include your unique selling points.

Your solutions are the Features, Advantages, and Benefits used to set the criteria. In a side-by-side table, you now explain how you can meet the prospect's specifications and the criteria you established.

4. **Present Financial Investment.** This is the Comparison Balance Sheet developed during the Effects/Consequences Questions. Here, you will show how your solution, which includes your unique selling points, has a significantly lower impact on the bottom line.

5. **Present the Plan of Action.** This comes from the Triggering Events Questions and the Interim Action Plan. This will include a specific structure to support half the buying populations' personality-based method of causing

or allowing a sale to complete.

Summary

The **Value Selling Strategies P.R.O.S.P.E.C.T Model (VSS)** was created to put each of the 10 Buyer Beliefs in place, thereby PREVENTING the objections that would come if this wasn't accomplished. The VSS is a "matrix" model that supports combining questions and using them in almost any sequence imaginable. With just a few well-targeted question combinations, you can take an hour meeting and reduce it to just a few minutes.

The **Customer Value Proposition** enables you to reinforce the "irrefutable logic" upon which the VSS is master. The Benefits question pulls in the emotional defense necessary to lock in your USP as minimal requirements to do business. If they are unique, meaning the competitor does not have them, and if they are set and locked in as criteria, then the competitor will not be able to meet the customer's needs in these areas.

About the Author

Dr. Robert "Bob" DeGroot, M.Ed., D.C.H., is the founder of Sales Training International. He is an author, counselor, consultant, sales professional, and trainer with over 30 years of experience in sales, training, and psychology.

He earned a Bachelor's in Psychology, Master of Education in School Psychology from Texas State University, and a Doctor of Clinical Hypnotherapy from the American Institute of Hypnotherapy.

He is the author of *Psychology for Successful Selling* (Branden Publishing Company, 1988) that launched the company. Bob has written over 70 training courses and 50 Web-based training courses and published dozens of bestselling eBooks in sales, sales management, and customer service.

Bob@SalesHelp.com

https://SalesHelp.com

Other books by Robert DeGroot

Sales Titles

Value Selling Strategies P.R.O.S.P.E.C.T. Model (Best Seller)
Strategic Sales Plan (Best Seller)
Objection Free Selling (Best Seller)
Features, Advantages, Benefits (Best Seller)
Negotiating Value
Benefit Questions Create Attitudes
Block the Competition
Trust & Rapport Building
Time & Territory Management
Goal Setting for Success (Best Seller)
Competitor Analysis
Closing Strategies of the Masters (Best Seller)

Sales Prospecting: The Hunt for New Business (includes the following short ebooks)

Profile and Qualify (Best Seller)
Key Decision Maker Roles (Best Seller)
Research Prospect & Competitor
Telephone Cold Call and Voicemail Strategies (Best Seller)
Email Prospecting (includes two bestsellers)
Networking Contact Strategy (Best Seller)
Asking for Referrals
Teleblitz (Best Seller)
Funnel Management (Best Seller)
Ratio Management (Best Seller)

Sales Management Titles

Reseller Strategy (Best Seller)
Career Path for Sales Professionals
Interviewing and Hiring

Sales Professionals Performance Appraisal
Sales Coach
Peer-to-Peer Sales Coaching (Best Seller)
Creating and Leading a Motivating Sales Culture
Effective Meeting Planning and Facilitating

Customer Service Titles

Telephone Etiquette for Business (Best Seller)
Active Listening Skills for Business (Best Seller)
Defusing Customer Anger
Problem-Solving Model for Business
Managing Customer Expectations (Best Seller)
E-mail Etiquette for Business
Stress Control at Work

You can connect with me on:

- https://bobdegroot.com
- https://www.saleshelp.com

www.ingramcontent.com/pod-product-compliance
Lightning Source LLC
LaVergne TN
LVHW010924110826
845149LV00013B/2468

* 9 7 8 0 9 8 6 4 0 5 8 9 1 *